DECORATING THE BATHROOM

103 Projects & Ideas

The Home Decorating Institute®

CONTENTS

Decorating the Bathroom

Shower & Window Curtains

Fabric Accessories

More Accessories

DECORATING THE BATHROOM

*Give the bathroom a face-lift
with a fresh decorating scheme
and well-chosen accessories.*

You can update the bathroom and make it more
functional without changing the size or layout of
the room. By redecorating, you can make dramatic
changes, yet avoid extensive remodeling costs. Sew
a new shower curtain, and you are on your way.

To make the bathroom look its best, stock it with
carefully selected accessories that soothe and serve
you. For the look of luxury, simple terry towels can be
easily transformed into elegant accessories by trimming
them with lace edgings, bands of contrasting fabrics,
appliqués, or monograms. Pamper yourself with bath
oils you prepared yourself and with your own blend
of potpourri.

On the practical side, you can increase your storage
space in creative new ways, perhaps using picnic
baskets for towels and toiletries. Or build a simple
storage unit or shelf. For aesthetics, create a floral
swag from silk flowers or a European container
garden of live plants.

*All information in this book has been tested; however,
because skill levels and conditions vary, the publisher
disclaims any liability for unsatisfactory results. Follow
the manufacturers' instructions for tools and materials
used to complete these projects. The publisher is not
responsible for any injury or damage caused by the
improper use of tools, materials, or information in
this publication.*

TYPES OF BATHROOMS

Bathrooms vary greatly, from small powder rooms to large, luxurious master baths. Your home may have a single bathroom or several. If you have more than one bathroom, you may designate one to be used by the children or reserve one as a guest bathroom.

The accessories you choose depend primarily on the type of bathroom you are decorating. For example, in a guest bathroom or powder room, you may accessorize with specialty soaps, decorative bath oils, potpourri, and fancy towels embellished with lace trims. Or in a child's bathroom, you may choose to decorate with a beach theme, with sand pails and beach balls as bathtime toys and using generous-size beach towels instead of ordinary bath towels.

THE MASTER BATHROOM

Whenever a bathroom is adjacent to the master bedroom, the decor usually matches or coordinates with the bedroom. Because this bathroom can become your private retreat, you may want to decorate it with colors that make you feel refreshed and soothed.

Often the largest bathroom in the house, the master bath may offer an opportunity to be more creative with furnishings, perhaps adding a vanity table or storage chest.

Projects from this book include: *fringed rug (page 65); monogrammed towel (page 74); towel displays (page 80); citrus-blend potpourri (page 96); decorated soaps (page 100); bath oil (page 104).*

THE GUEST BATHROOM

If your house has a guest bath, you may want
to accessorize it thoughtfully with items that
will make your guests feel welcome, such
as special guest towels and a basketful of
toiletries. You may even want to hang a
bathrobe on a hook. If you like the look
of some of the higher-maintenance materials,
like brass, the guest bathroom may be a good
place to use them, because this room is not used
on a daily basis.

Projects from this book include: *basic
shower curtain (page 26); sink skirt (page 61);
lace-trimmed towels (page 79); towel displays
(page 80); decorating with toiletries (page 100);
guest box (page 102); floral swag (page 118).*

TYPES OF BATHROOMS (CONTINUED)

THE POWDER ROOM

Often referred to as a half bath, a powder room usually lacks a bathtub or shower, making it the smallest of bathrooms. But, just because it is small, a powder room does not have to lack charm. Use a small bathroom as an opportunity to splurge on luxurious materials that are unaffordable in the larger quantities required elsewhere. Or try a bolder, more adventurous color scheme and decor than you would feel comfortable using in a large space. You can make the bathroom appear larger by continuing the color scheme of the adjacent room, especially if light colors are used. Another way to add visual size to the room is to use large or multiple mirrors and glass shelves instead of wooden shelves.

Projects from this book include: fabric-covered wastebasket (page 92); container garden (page 123); rose-blend potpourri (page 96); framed mirror (page 88); decorated soaps (page 100); decorative bath oils (page 104).

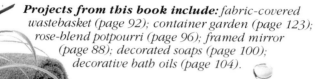

THE CHILDREN'S BATHROOM

When children have their own bathroom filled with bright colors and cheerful objects, bathtime is no longer a chore. Consider how you will be able to adapt the room for a new look as the children grow older and their tastes change. For example, an all-white bathroom can be furnished in bright crayon colors for young children, but can be redecorated later by simply replacing the accessories.

Because safety is especially important in children's bathrooms, use slip-resistant flooring and rubber tub mats. Furnish a one-step stool that is skidproof, but keep items within easy reach, when possible, to avoid unnecessary climbing. To prevent burning a child with hot water, use anti-scald plumbing fittings that inhibit the flow of hot water when the temperature exceeds a predetermined point. They are sold at hardware stores and home centers, and you can easily install them yourself.

Projects from this book include: *towels with reverse appliqué (page 74); decoupage wastebasket (page 92); painted medicine cabinet (page 21); rod-pocket curtains (page 31); braided tiebacks (page 36).*

SELECTING
A STYLE

Whether you are decorating a master bath, a guest bath, or a powder room, it can reflect your tastes in decorating. For a country bathroom, you may choose simple bathroom furnishings, such as muslin shower and window curtains, a skirted pedestal sink, and a braided rug. For a contemporary bathroom, select sleek accessories, such as a tailored shower valance over the shower doors, a contemporary frame for the vanity mirror, and a clean-lined wastebasket. You may choose to work around a theme when you plan the bathroom decorating scheme. For example, you may want to try a woodland or nature theme that is centered around birdhouses and twig baskets. Or try a beach theme, accessorizing with seashells.

Traditional style *(left) shows off elegant accessories like brass swag holders. Here, the swag holders are used as towel rings to hold towels folded jabot-style (page 81). An elegant picture frame is used to frame a mirror (page 88). Silk flowers (page 118), rose-blend potpourri (page 96), and appliquéd towels (page 74) carry out the style.*

Victorian look *begins with the use of a skirted vanity table (page 61). Delicate perfume bottles are arranged on an intricate mirror tray (page 88), and potpourri in a rose blend (page 96) is arranged in a porcelain bowl. For that special guest, wrap toiletries in a pretty gift box (page 102).*

Contemporary style *incorporates clean-lined furnishings. A simple fabric-covered wastebasket (page 92) is sewn in an abstract print. A bin-and-shelving unit (page 112), a framed mirror (page 88), and medallion towel holders (page 84) are all painted in bright gold for a contemporary look.*

Country style *is reflected in simple accessories like a picket fence box (page 107) and a nest of bath soaps (page 103). Rod-pocket curtains (page 31) with braided tiebacks (page 34) are sewn in basic cotton.*

Woodland look *(right) is pulled together with rustic materials and a collection of small birdhouses. A birch-bark basket is used for a container garden (page 123); pine-forest potpourri (page 96) and decorated soaps (page 100) add a finishing touch.*

SELECTING COLORS & PATTERNS

The decorating style you have chosen may help you decide which colors and patterns to use in the bathroom, because certain colors and patterns tend to be associated with traditional, country, and contemporary decorating schemes. For example, burgundy cabbage roses are usually associated with traditional decorating, Wedgwood blue miniprints with country decorating, and Southwest colors in abstract patterns with contemporary decorating.

When selecting colors and patterns, consider the size of the bathroom and the final effect you are striving for. A small bathroom appears larger when decorated in light colors, but can be charming and cozy when deep, dark colors are used. If you are installing new tiles and fixtures, it is advisable to use neutral colors that can stand the test of time. But the bathroom does offer an excellent opportunity to use trendier colors in accessories, such as shower curtains, towels, and rugs, which can be easily and inexpensively replaced as trends and tastes change.

In solid colors and patterns, the fabrics selected for curtains, towels, and rugs soften the look of a bathroom. Wallcoverings can add interest and are an excellent way to introduce a pattern.

Patterns can be formal or casual, serious or fun, subtle or bold. To add spunk to the decorating scheme, you may want to combine patterns. For best results, choose patterns that share a common color, yet differ in scale, perhaps mixing striped fabrics with florals.

WORKING AROUND EXISTING COLORS IN TILES & FIXTURES

You may find it necessary to base the color scheme of the bathroom on existing fixtures or surfaces that you are not replacing, such as outdated tiles or a colored porcelain tub, sink, and toilet.

If the existing surfaces are pastel or neutral, you can draw attention away from them by introducing stronger or brighter colors in the room. For example, if the porcelain fixtures are mint green, you might select a patterned wallcovering that is predominately forest green. If the existing colors are bright, you can soften their impact with the addition of calm colors; however, you will want to use bright colors in small, fun accessories to tie the look together.

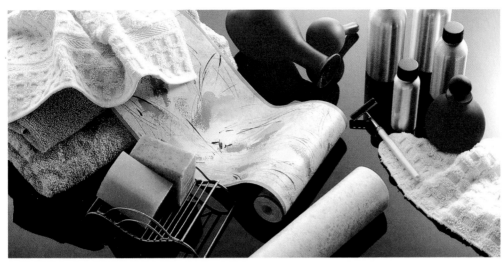

Bright porcelain fixtures, *such as cobalt blue, are combined with neutrals. To tie in the bold fixtures, add small accessories in the bright blue.*

Color sample represents the existing bright blue porcelain fixtures.

Pastel porcelain fixtures, *such as a mint green tub, sink, and toilet, draw less attention when combined with a brighter or darker shade of the same color. Shown here, darker greens have been used with mint green fixtures; yellow accessories are used as accents.*

Color sample represents the existing mint green porcelain fixtures.

Gray plastic tiles *may be minimized by combining them with striking colors. Shown here, black, white, and red are used to accessorize the bathroom, with touches of gray in the wallcovering.*

Color sample represents the existing gray tiles.

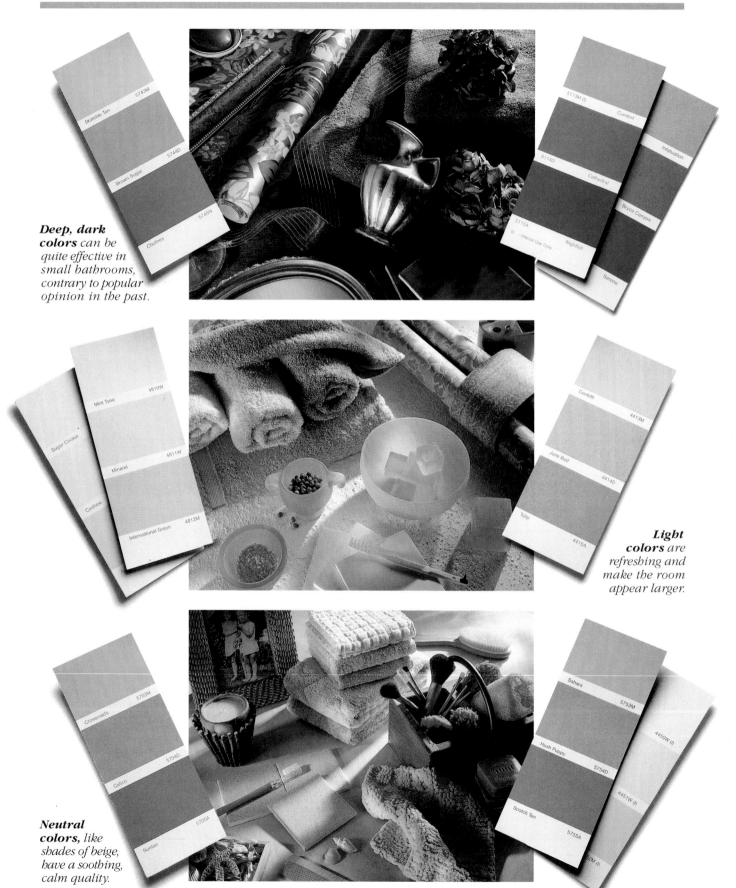

Deep, dark colors *can be quite effective in small bathrooms, contrary to popular opinion in the past.*

Light colors *are refreshing and make the room appear larger.*

Neutral colors, *like shades of beige, have a soothing, calm quality.*

Pastel patterns and blonde wood add a soft, feminine look. Wicker adds texture.

Bright colors will contrast with white porcelain fixtures and tiles to make the room bold and cheerful.

Strong colors and patterns in a bathroom have a masculine effect.

CERAMIC TILE DESIGN

Available in many colors, shapes, and sizes, ceramic tile promises limitless design possibilities. If you are having new tiles installed, there are many design options to choose from. You may want to use creative borders and tile designs to give the bathroom a look that is unique.

For long-term practicality, select neutrals or whites, since the use of tiles in trendy colors decreases the value of a home over time. If a color accent is desired, smaller amounts of colored tiles in a classic color may be used, perhaps in a border design.

Narrow bars *frame the edges of wall tile.*

Alternating colors *are used for this tile border.*

Diamond design border (above) *creates interest without becoming overwhelming.*

Random placement *of tiles (below) in three coordinating colors has an unstructured look.*

Diagonal lines *of a countertop or floor make an effective presentation for simple ivory tiles.*

Hand-painted tiles (below) *make a bathroom unique.*

BATHROOM STORAGE IDEAS

The storage space in the bathroom is usually under the sink or in a linen closet with deep shelves. To utilize these spaces efficiently, it is helpful to install pull-out drawers and other cabinet organizers. However, since many bathrooms have limited cabinet and closet space, it is often necessary to create additional storage space. Skirt a wall-mounted sink or vanity table (page 61) to add concealed storage. Or build shelves, such as the picket fence shelves on page 107 or the bin-and-shelving units on page 112, for the convenient storage of bath oils and cosmetics and for extra display space. Baskets, Shaker boxes, and hat boxes also provide storage and make attractive bathroom accessories.

Three stacked picnic baskets, *tucked in a corner, offer extra, convenient storage for towels. Smaller baskets can be used on the countertop to organize cosmetics, jewelry, and other items.*

Collection of Shaker boxes (right) adds charm to a country bathroom, while providing storage for small items.

Old-fashioned pie safe (right) stores linens and cleaning supplies. The tall cabinet requires minimal space. An old wooden bucket also provides storage.

(Continued)

BATHROOM STORAGE IDEAS <small>(CONTINUED)</small>

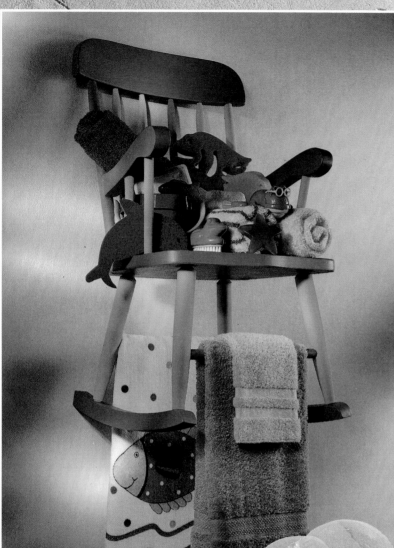

Mesh bag stores children's bath toys. Hung conveniently in the shower area, the bag allows toys to dry between uses.

Child's rocking chair (left), hung on the wall, provides creative storage space. The chair seat serves as a shelf, and the crossbars become towel holders. The runners were shortened to allow the chair to hang level.

Tub tray (below) is convenient for keeping soap and other bath items within easy reach.

Unfinished medicine cabinets, *available at unpainted wood furniture stores, can be decoratively painted for a whimsical look.*

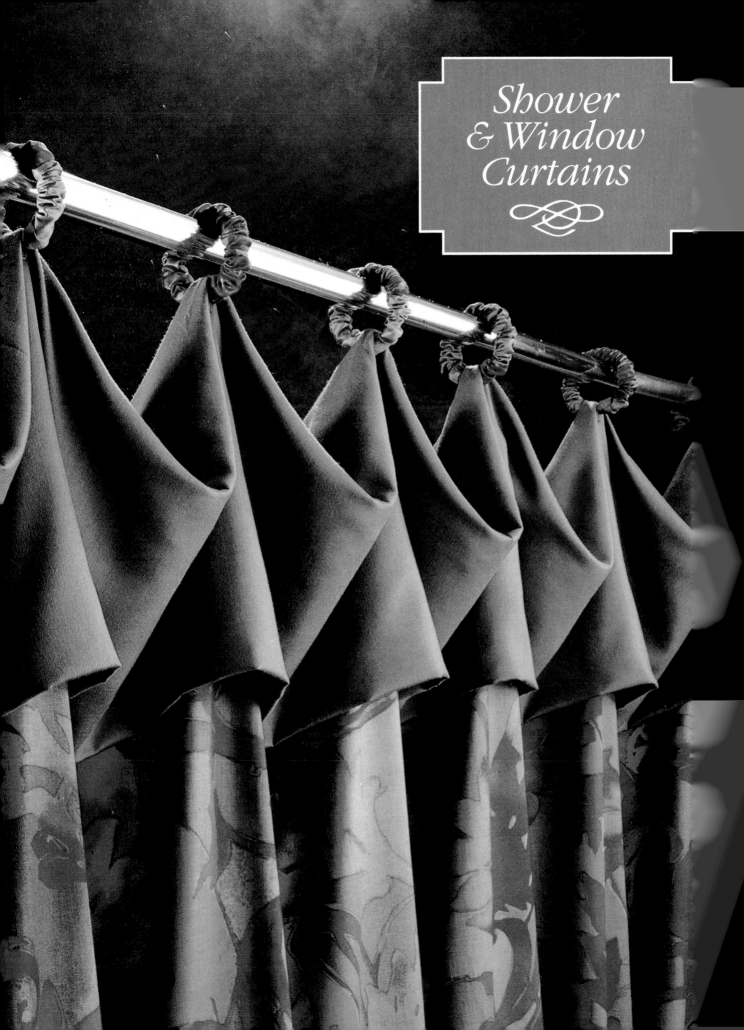

Shower & Window Curtains

CURTAIN HARDWARE

When you are choosing the type of shower curtains and window treatments you want for the bathroom, also consider the selection of hardware that is available. You may want to use shiny chrome or brass hardware to carry out the look of the faucets and other fixtures. Or, for an old-world or country look, select wooden poles that coordinate with wooden toilet tanks and seats. Consider whether the curtain will be hung from rings, allowing the rod to show, or if the rod will be concealed by inserting it into a rod-pocket curtain.

Determine where the rod will be mounted, in order to make sure the correct mounting brackets are purchased.

The rods for window treatments are often used with a pair of wall-mount brackets that project out from the wall. Shower bars are usually installed between the side walls of the shower opening by using a rod with socket-style brackets or a spring-tension rod without brackets.

If the brackets will be installed on a ceramic tile wall, you may drill into the ceramic tile with a glass-and-tile drill bit and insert a plastic anchor into the hole before you install the bracket. Or use an adhesive mounting plate, shown opposite, to eliminate the need for drilling into the ceramic tile. Adhesive plastic hooks are also available for use as tieback holders on ceramic tile walls.

CURTAIN RODS & SHOWER BARS

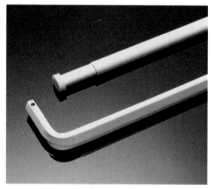

Oval curtain rods, 1" (2.5 cm) wide, are used to hang rod-pocket window treatments. For rod-pocket shower curtains, spring-tension oval rods are also available.

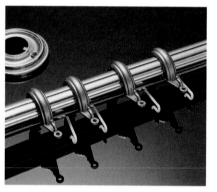

Dual-channel shower bars allow the outer curtain and the liner to slide independently on separate tracks. For the outer curtain, the rings ride in the front track; for the liner, the slides ride in the back.

Shower bars, sold with end plates, are available in brass and chrome. The end plates are screwed into the side walls of the shower opening.

Wide curtain rods are available in both 2½" and 4½" (6.5 and 11.5 cm) widths. They add depth and interest to rod-pocket window treatments. Both these widths are available in wall-mount rods for window treatments and in spring-tension rods for shower curtains.

Round spring-tension rods are available in several diameters and finishes. They may be used for shower curtains or inside-mounted window treatments, such as cafe curtains. Because no mounting brackets are needed, the window frames and shower walls are not damaged by screws.

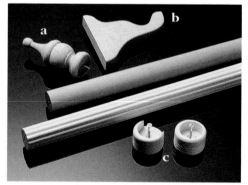

Wooden poles are available unfinished and in several finishes. For a window treatment, finials **(a)** are attached to the ends of the pole, and wooden brackets **(b)** are used for mounting the pole. When used as a shower bar, the pole is mounted with wooden sockets **(c);** these sockets may be stained or painted to match the pole. Wooden rings are also available (opposite).

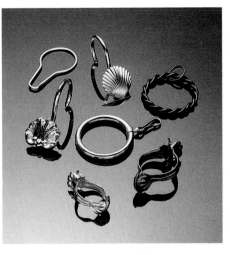

Fabric-covered rings can be purchased in a limited selection of fabrics. They are also easy to make as on page 40, using fabric that coordinates with the shower curtain.

Metal rings and hooks, sold in sets of twelve, are available in brass, nickel, iron, and chrome. The styles range from simple utility rings to ornamental designs.

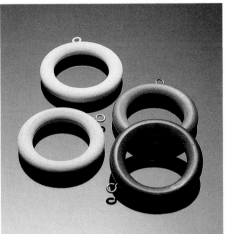

Wooden rings can be used as shower curtain rings with a wooden pole. They may also be used for window curtains hung from a wooden pole. The rings may be stained or painted to match the pole.

Molded plastic rings, available in several colors, snap open and closed. They are also sold in sets of twelve.

ACCESSORIES

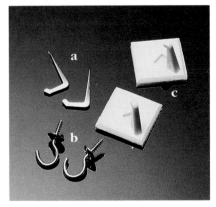

Adhesive mounting kits are used to mount shower bars, making it unnecessary to drill holes in ceramic tiles. The mounting plate is affixed to the tile with a double-stick adhesive disk, and the rod brackets screw into the plate.

Plastic covers for shower bars are available in several colors, to match plastic shower curtain rings. The cover allows the rings to slide easily when the curtain is drawn. Cut the cover to the exact length with scissors.

Tieback holders are used to keep the tiebacks of shower curtains and window treatments in place. For mounting on drywall or woodwork, use either tenter hooks **(a)** or cup hooks **(b).** For mounting on ceramic tile, use adhesive plastic hooks **(c).**

BASIC SHOWER CURTAINS

By sewing a shower curtain instead of purchasing one ready-made, you have more flexibility in fabric selection. Make a basic curtain that matches or coordinates with the fabrics in an adjoining bedroom. Or make shower and window curtains in complementary styles and matching fabrics.

The basic shower curtain has grommets or buttonholes at the top, spaced to match the holes along the top of a shower curtain liner, so that the curtain and liner can be hung together on the same rod. A separate valance, constructed like the curtain, may be added and hung together with the curtain and liner. Or the valance may be attached to the shower curtain.

A basic shower curtain measures 72" (183 cm) long and 72" (183 cm) wide, to be used with a standard liner, and is usually mounted so the lower edge is about 2" (5 cm) from the floor. The curtain can be made longer than 72"

(183 cm), if desired, but, to ensure that the curtain and liner hang together properly, do not alter the width.

For easy laundering, choose a fabric that is washable, preshrinking it before sewing the curtain by washing and drying the fabric according to the manufacturer's directions. Avoid using decorator fabrics with polished finishes, because they are usually not washable and any water that is splashed on the decorator fabric can leave noticeable spots.

MATERIALS

- 4⅝ yd. (4.25 m) fabric; allow extra fabric for matching patterned fabric.
- Twelve grommets and attaching tool, optional.
- Shower curtain liner.
- Shower bar and twelve rings.

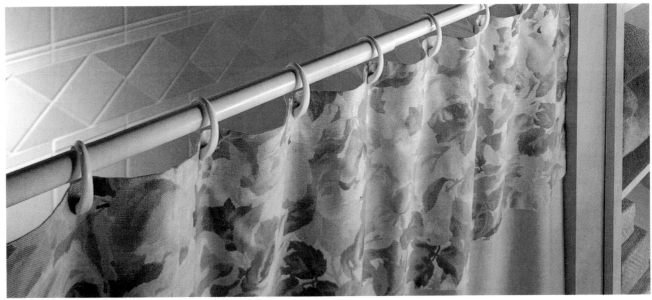

Basic shower curtains may be used alone, as shown opposite, or with either a separate or an attached valance. The valance above, sewn from a contrasting fabric, is stitched to the top of the curtain.

HOW TO SEW A BASIC SHOWER CURTAIN WITH AN OPTIONAL SEPARATE VALANCE

CUTTING DIRECTIONS

For the shower curtain, cut two lengths of fabric, 10" (25.5 cm) longer than the desired finished length; for a standard 72" (183 cm) finished length, the cut length is 82" (208.5 cm). Seam the fabric widths together, using a French seam, as in steps 1 to 3; or use a conventional seam and omit steps 1 to 3. Trim one side so the cut width of the shower curtain is 76" (193 cm), or 4" (10 cm) wider than the desired finished width.

For a separate valance, cut two lengths of fabric, 6" (15 cm) longer than the desired finished length; the finished length of most valances is about 15" (38 cm). Seam the fabric widths together, using a French seam, and trim the valance to the same cut width as the shower curtain.

1 Pin fabric widths for curtain panel, *wrong* sides together; stitch scant ¼" (6 mm) seam. Press seam allowances to one side.

(Continued)

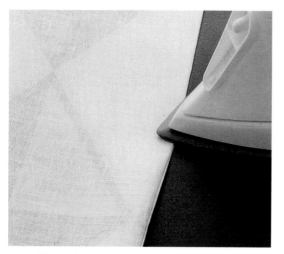

2 Fold the fabric along the seamline, right sides together, enclosing seam allowances; press.

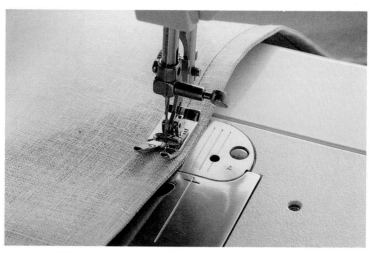

3 Stitch ⅜" (1 cm) from folded edge, enclosing first seam. Press French seam to one side.

4 Trim curtain panel to 76" (193 cm) wide, or 4" (10 cm) wider than the desired finished width, trimming one side of the panel. Press under 3" (7.5 cm) twice on lower edge of curtain panel; stitch to make 3" (7.5 cm) double-fold hem. Press under 1" (2.5 cm) twice on each side of the curtain panel; stitch to make 1" (2.5 cm) double-fold side hems.

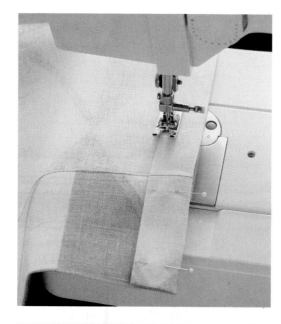

5 Press under and stitch 2" (5 cm) double-fold hem on upper edge of curtain panel.

6 Mark curtain panel for the placement of twelve buttonholes or grommets, a scant 6¼" (15.7 cm) apart and ¾" (2 cm) down from top, with end marks 1½" (3.8 cm) from the sides.

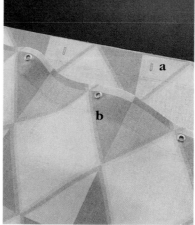

7 Make ½" (1.3 cm) buttonholes **(a),** if desired, stitching them vertically with upper ends at the placement marks. Or fasten grommets **(b)** securely, following the manufacturer's directions, centering the grommets on the placement marks.

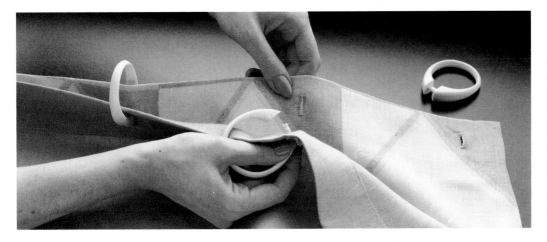

Valance. Construct the valance as on pages 27 and 28, steps 1 to 7, except, in step 4, press and stitch a 1" (2.5 cm) double-fold lower hem. Attach shower curtain rings to tops of curtain and valance, through both layers as shown.

HOW TO SEW A BASIC SHOWER CURTAIN WITH AN ATTACHED VALANCE

CUTTING DIRECTIONS

For the shower curtain, cut two lengths of fabric, 6" (15 cm) longer than the desired finished length; for a standard 72" (183 cm) finished length, the cut length is 78" (198 cm). Seam the fabric widths together as necessary, using a French seam, as on pages 27 and 28, steps 1 to 3; or use a conventional seam. Trim one side so the cut width of the shower curtain is 76" (193 cm), or 4" (10 cm) wider than the desired finished width. For the attached valance, cut two lengths of fabric, 4½" (11.5 cm) longer than the desired finished length of the valance; the finished length of most valances is about 15" (38 cm). Seam the fabric widths together, using a French seam, and trim the valance to the same width as the shower curtain.

1 Seam fabric widths together for curtain panel and for valance panel; if desired, stitch French seam as on pages 27 and 28, steps 1 to 3. Follow step 4, opposite, for curtain panel; for the valance, follow step 4, except press and stitch 1" (2.5 cm) double-fold lower hem. On upper edge of valance, press under ½" (1.3 cm), then 2" (5 cm).

2 Place the valance right side down on flat surface. Place curtain right side down over valance, with upper edge of the curtain even with folded edge of the valance; pin in place.

3 Stitch along lower fold, catching the curtain between layers of valance.

4 Mark and apply buttonholes or grommets as in steps 6 and 7, opposite.

Valance and cafe curtains, with their casual style, are appropriate for a country bathroom. On a double-hung window, mount the curtain rod for the cafe curtain above the center of the window.

ROD-POCKET CURTAINS & VALANCES

Rod-pocket curtains are simple-to-sew panels of fabric that are gathered as they are fed onto a curtain rod. Often unlined for a soft, lightweight look, they can be used as either shower curtains or window treatments. For more interest at the top of the curtain, a separate or attached valance may be added.

Rod-pocket shower curtains are stationary, often held in place with tiebacks. A second rod is used for the shower curtain liner, allowing it to be opened and closed. When a valance is desired, it is attached to the curtain itself (page 33), to eliminate the need for a third rod.

Tieback curtains may also be used at the window. Or you may choose cafe curtains and a valance. The cafes offer privacy by covering the lower portion of the window, and the valance completes the look at the top of the window.

Tieback shower curtains (opposite) add softness to a tiled bathroom. Because rod-pocket curtains are stationary, the shower liner is hung on a separate rod, allowing it to be pulled closed. Shown here with an attached valance, the curtain may also be sewn without a valance.

Tieback curtains give a small window a perky look. Although the curtains are shown here without a valance, one may be added, using the method for either an attached or a separate valance.

HOW TO SEW A ROD-POCKET CURTAIN OR VALANCE

MATERIALS

• Fabric.   • Curtain rod.

CUTTING DIRECTIONS

Determine the desired finished length of the curtain or valance from the top of the heading to the hemmed lower edge. Also decide on the depth of the rod pocket and heading and the depth of the lower hem. The rod pocket is one-half the measurement around the rod plus ¼" (6 mm); lower hems may be 3" (7.5 cm) for shower and window curtains and 2" (5 cm) for a valance.

The cut length of the fabric is equal to the desired finished length of the curtain plus the depth of the heading and the rod pocket, ½" (1.3 cm) for turn-under at the upper edge, and twice the hem depth.

Determine the cut width of the fabric by multiplying the length of the rod by two and one-half; if you are sewing two curtain panels, divide this measurement by two, to determine the cut width of each panel. For each panel, add 4" (10 cm) to allow for two 1" (2.5 cm) double-fold side hems; also add 1" (2.5 cm) for each seam. Seam the fabric widths together as necessary; if desired, stitch French seams as on pages 27 and 28, steps 1 to 3.

1 Seam the fabric widths together as necessary for each curtain panel or for the valance; if desired, stitch French seams as on pages 27 and 28, steps 1 to 3. At lower edge, press under the hem allowance twice to wrong side; stitch hem.

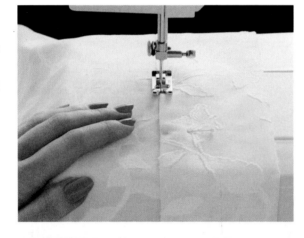

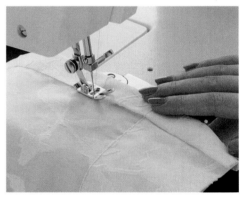

2 Press under 1" (2.5 cm) twice on sides; stitch hems.

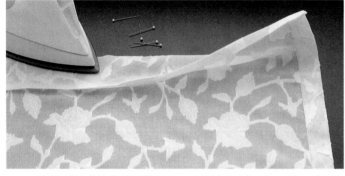

3 Press under ½" (1.3 cm) on upper edge. Then press under an amount equal to rod-pocket depth plus heading depth.

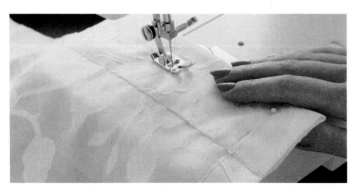

4 Stitch close to the first fold. Stitch again at depth of heading, using tape on bed of machine as stitching guide.

5 Insert curtain rod through rod pocket, gathering fabric evenly. Hang curtain or valance.

HOW TO SEW A ROD-POCKET CURTAIN
WITH AN ATTACHED VALANCE

MATERIALS

• Fabric.   • Curtain rod.

CUTTING DIRECTIONS

Determine the desired finished length of the curtain from the top of the heading to the hemmed lower edge. Also decide on the depth of the rod pocket and the heading. The rod pocket is one-half the measurement around the rod plus ¼" (6 mm); lower hems may be 3" (7.5 cm) for shower and window curtains and 2" (5 cm) for a valance.

The cut length of the fabric for the curtain panels is equal to the desired finished length of the curtain plus twice the hem depth. Determine the cut width of the fabric for the curtain panels by multiplying the length of the rod by two and one-half; if you are sewing two curtain panels, divide this measurement by two to determine the cut width of each panel. For each panel, add 4" (10 cm) to allow for two 1" (2.5 cm) double-fold side hems; if it is necessary to piece fabric widths together, also add 1" (2.5 cm) for each seam.

Determine the desired finished length of the valance from the top of the heading to the hemmed lower edge. The cut length of the fabric for the valance is equal to the desired finished length of the valance plus the depth of the heading and rod pocket, ½" (1.3 cm) for turn-under at the upper edge, and twice the hem depth.

The cut width of the valance is equal to the finished width of the curtain plus 4" (10 cm) for the side hems; also add 1" (2.5 cm) for each seam. If two curtain panels are to be attached to the same valance, base the cut width of the valance on the combined finished width of the curtain panels.

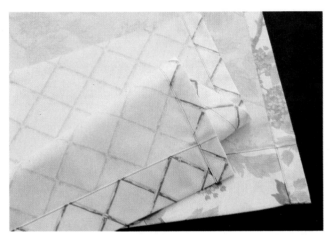

1 Seam fabric widths and stitch the lower and side hems of the curtain panels and valance as in steps 1 and 2, opposite.

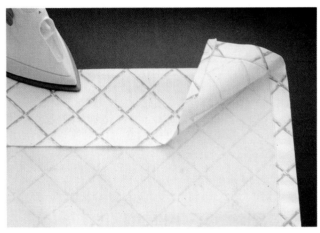

2 Press under ½" (1.3 cm) on upper edge of the valance. Then press under an amount equal to the rod-pocket depth plus heading depth.

3 Place the valance right side down on a flat surface; open out upper fold. Place the curtain panels over valance, right side down, aligning upper edge of curtain with foldline on valance. Refold the upper edge of the valance, encasing upper edge of curtain; pin in place.

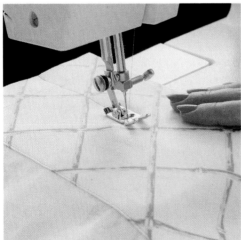

4 Stitch the rod pocket as in step 4, opposite; hang curtain as in step 5.

Braided tiebacks (above) can repeat the design and colors of a braided rug (page 70).

Shirred tiebacks (left) mimic the effect created at the heading of rod pocket curtains (page 31).

Many rod-pocket curtains are used with tiebacks that hold the panels in place. Tiebacks offer a decorative opportunity to repeat a design or embellishment used elsewhere in the bathroom. For example, the design of a braided rug (page 70) can be repeated in a braided tieback, or the shirred effect created by the rod pocket can be repeated in a shirred tieback. You may want to sew fabric bands or galloon lace onto tiebacks with tucked ends, to coordinate with decorative towels (pages 74 and 75) or shower curtains (pages 56 and 57).

Braided or shirred tiebacks can be made from covered cording. Consider the size of the window or shower curtain when choosing the size of the cording. Because these tiebacks are circular, they

Tiebacks with tucked ends *have clean, simple design lines. Above, coordinating fabrics are used for the shower curtain and tieback. At right, the tieback is trimmed with fabric bands as on page 78.*

can simply be slipped onto the curtain from the bottom and secured with one hook. For tiebacks with tucked ends, apply mediumweight fusible interfacing to the wrong side of the fabric for added body.

The position of the tiebacks on the window curtain affects the amount of exposed glass as well as the overall look of the curtains. Position tiebacks low to cover more of the window and to visually widen the window. If tiebacks are positioned high, more of the glass is exposed and visual height is added to the window. Also follow these guidelines for positioning the tiebacks on a shower curtain, allowing enough room for easy access to the tub.

HOW TO MAKE BRAIDED TIEBACKS

MATERIALS

- Fabrics in one, two, or three solid colors or prints.
- Cording in desired diameter.
- Sew-on or pin-on tieback rings.

CUTTING DIRECTIONS

Determine the finished circumference of the tieback by pulling back the curtain at the desired location with a flexible tape measure. For one braided tieback, cut three lengths of cording, each three times the finished circumference of the tieback; wrap tape around the ends to prevent fraying. Cut three fabric strips, each one and one-half times the finished circumference of the tieback; to determine the width of the fabric strips, measure around the cording and add 1" (2.5 cm).

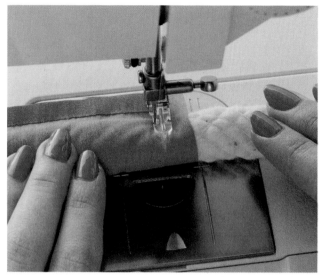

1 Fold one fabric strip around one length of the cording, right sides together, matching the raw edges. Using a zipper foot, stitch loosely along the cording from one end of the fabric strip to the other; do not crowd the cording. Pivot, and stitch across fabric strip, about ½" (1.3 cm) from end of fabric, sewing through middle of cording length.

2 Hold fabric loosely at stitched end; pull the fabric from covered to uncovered end of cording, turning the tube right side out to encase the cording. Cut off the cording just beyond stitched end; discard excess cording. Repeat to cover the remaining cords; three cords are needed for each braided tieback.

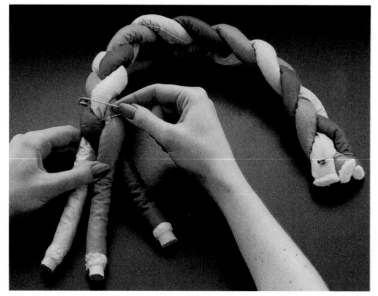

3 Pin the three covered cords together, about 1" (2.5 cm) from the stitched ends, using large safety pin. Braid loosely to desired length, keeping seams to back of braid. Measure from end of cords to 1" (2.5 cm) less than desired finished circumference, and pin cords together at that point with another safety pin.

4 Shape the braid into a circle; cut cords at end of braid so they overlap cords at beginning of braid by 1" (2.5 cm). Pull out and cut off 1" (2.5 cm) of cording from each cut end; slide end of fabric tube back over end of the cording.

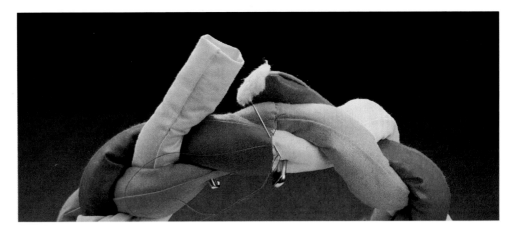

5 Turn under ½" (1.3 cm) of fabric at ends of tubes. Insert stitched ends of the covered cords into open ends of the fabric tubes, overlapping ½" (1.3 cm) and joining ends so braid is continuous; slipstitch. Remove safety pins. Attach a tieback ring.

HOW TO MAKE SHIRRED TIEBACKS

MATERIALS

- Fabric that matches or contrasts with curtain fabric.
- Cording in desired diameter.
- Sew-on or pin-on tieback rings.

CUTTING DIRECTIONS

For each tieback, cut a length of cording equal to three times the finished circumference of the tieback; wrap tape around the ends to prevent fraying. Cut a fabric strip equal to twice the finished circumference of the tieback; to determine the width of the fabric strip, measure around the cording and add 2" (5 cm).

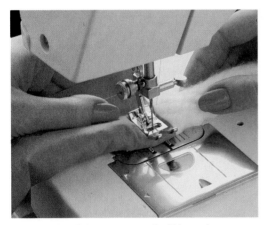

1 Fold the fabric strip in half lengthwise, right sides together, encasing the cording; stitch a ½" (1.3 cm) seam. Stitch across the end of the fabric strip through cording.

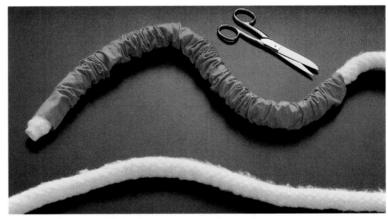

2 Hold fabric loosely at stitched end; pull fabric from the covered to the uncovered end of cording, turning tube right side out to encase the cording and gathering fabric as tube is turned. Cut off and discard excess cording.

3 Sew the ends of the cording together securely.

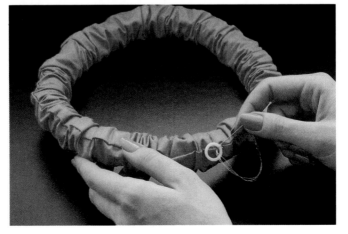

4 Turn under ½" (1.3 cm) at the end of the fabric tube. Overlap the stitched end of the covered cord; slipstitch in place. Distribute fabric evenly along the cording. Attach a tieback ring.

HOW TO SEW TIEBACKS WITH TUCKED ENDS

MATERIALS

- Fabric that matches or contrasts with the curtain fabric.
- Fusible interfacing.
- Sew-on or pin-on tieback rings.
- Optional embellishments, such as fabric bands (page 78) or galloon lace (page 79).

CUTTING DIRECTIONS

For each tieback, cut a fabric strip 1" (2.5 cm) longer than the desired finished length, with the width of the fabric strip equal to twice the desired finished width plus 1" (2.5 cm). Cut a strip of fusible interfacing to the desired finished length and width of the tieback.

1 Center strip of fusible interfacing on the wrong side of fabric strip, and fuse in place, following the manufacturer's directions. The right side of the interfaced area will be the front of the tieback.

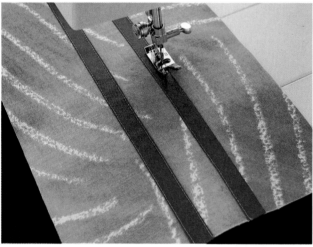

2 Apply any desired embellishments to right side of the tieback in the interfaced area, such as the fabric bands (page 78) shown.

3 Fold the tieback in half, right sides together. Stitch ½" (1.3 cm) lengthwise seam, leaving opening for turning. Press seam open.

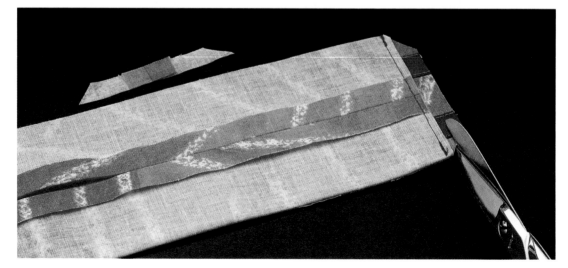

4 Center seam on back of tieback. Stitch ½" (1.3 cm) seams at the ends; trim seam allowances, and clip corners.

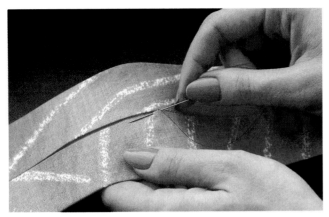

5 Turn the tieback right side out, and press. Slipstitch the opening closed.

6 Fold one end of the tieback in half, right sides together. Stitch a tuck, 1" (2.5 cm) long and ⅜" (1 cm) from the fold, starting 1" (2.5 cm) from end of tieback. Repeat for opposite end.

7 Flatten the tuck, centering it over the stitches.

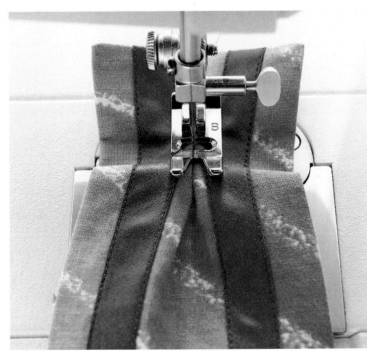

8 Stitch in the ditch of the tuck from the right side, to hold it in place. Repeat for opposite end.

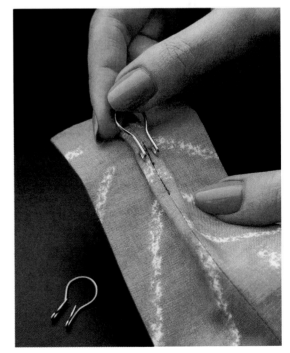

9 Attach pin-on tieback rings as shown. Or stitch sew-on tieback rings in place.

SHIRRED
SHOWER RINGS

Plastic shower rings and wooden cafe rings may be covered with fabric to match or coordinate with a custom shower curtain. A stitched-and-turned fabric tube is gathered as you slide it around the ring. To cover a wooden ring, saw through the ring on one side to allow the fabric tube to be inserted.

To cover plastic shower rings, cut one 2¼" (6 cm) fabric strip for each ring; cut the strip 15" to 22" (38 to 56 cm) long, depending on the fabric weight. For lightweight fabrics, cut the strips longer than for heavier fabrics.

To cover wooden cafe rings, cut one 3" (7.5 cm) fabric strip for each ring; cut the strips 20" to 25" (51 to 63.5 cm) long, depending on the fabric weight.

HOW TO COVER A PLASTIC SHOWER RING WITH FABRIC

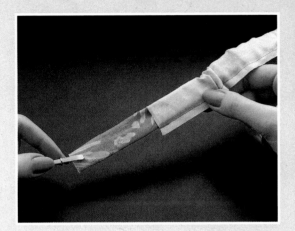

1 Fold 2¼" (6 cm) fabric strip in half lengthwise, right sides together; stitch ¼" (6 mm) seam. Turn fabric tube right side out, using bodkin or loop turner.

2 Open shower ring, and slide fabric tube around ring, gathering tightly.

HOW TO COVER A WOODEN CAFE RING WITH FABRIC

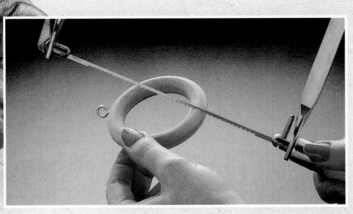

1 Follow step 1, above, using 3" (7.5 cm) fabric strip. Saw through one side of wooden cafe ring.

2 Remove the screw eye from the ring; slide fabric tube around ring.

3 Wrap the sawed opening in the ring with tape.

4 Slide fabric tube around ring to expose hole for screw eye. Replace screw eye in wooden ring.

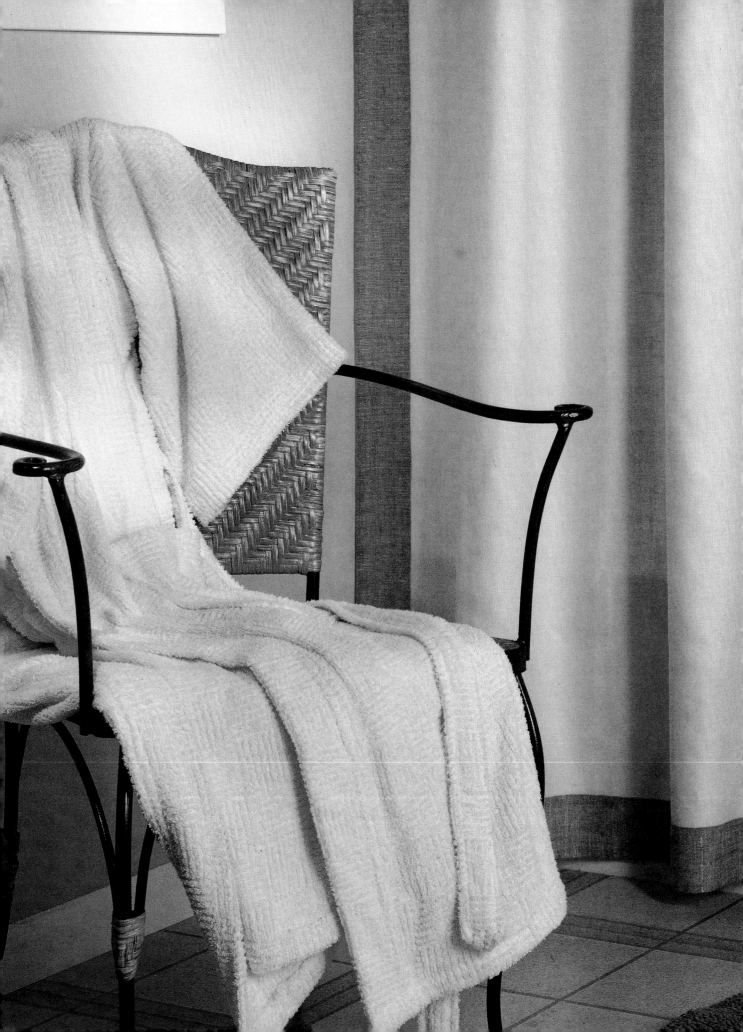

BANDED
SHOWER
CURTAINS

For a striking, tailored effect, make a shower curtain with contrasting banded edges. Combine two solid-colored fabrics to give a simple, yet dramatic, look. Or use a patterned fabric with a coordinating solid.

The instructions that follow are for a standard shower curtain that measures 72" (183 cm) long and 72" (183 cm) wide. The curtain can be hung together with a standard shower curtain liner, using one shower bar and one set of rings.

MATERIALS

- 4½ yd. (4.15 m) fabric, for the curtain.
- 2¼ yd. (2.1 m) fabric, for the bands.
- Twelve grommets and attaching tool, optional.
- Shower curtain liner.
- Shower bar and twelve rings.

CUTTING DIRECTIONS

For the curtain panel, cut two lengths of fabric, 76½" (194.3 cm) long; this allows for the seam allowance at the bottom and for the upper hem. Seam the fabric widths together; if desired, stitch a French seam as on pages 27 and 28, steps 1 to 3. Trim one side so the cut width of the curtain panel is 73" (185.5 cm); this allows for the seam allowances at the sides.

Cut two fabric strips for the side bands, 76½" (194.3 cm) long, and cut one fabric strip for the lower band, 73" (185.5 cm) long, cutting these strips on the lengthwise grain to eliminate any seams. The cut width of the fabric strips is 1" (2.5 cm) wider than the desired finished width of the band.

HOW TO SEW A BANDED SHOWER CURTAIN

1 Seam the fabric widths together. Trim curtain panel to 73" (185.5 cm) wide, trimming one side of the panel. Press under ½" (1.3 cm) on one long edge of one side band. Pin band to curtain panel, with right side of band to wrong side of panel. Stitch a ½" (1.3 cm) seam, stopping ½" (1.3 cm) from lower edge. Repeat for band on opposite side.

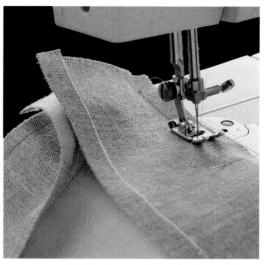

2 Press under ½" (1.3 cm) on one long edge of lower band. Pin to lower edge of curtain panel, with right side of band to wrong side of panel. Stitch ½" (1.3 cm) seam; start and stop ½" (1.3 cm) from side edges.

3 Mark band for mitering, placing pins at inner corner as shown.

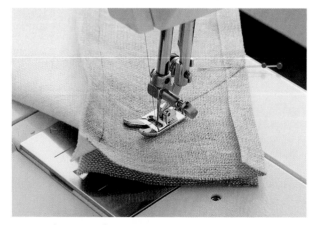

4 Stitch miters, from pin marks at inner corner to end of stitching at outer corner; take care not to catch the curtain panel in stitching.

5 Trim mitered seams to ¼" (6 mm), and press open. Trim the corners diagonally.

6 Press seams open by pressing seam allowance of band toward band, using tip of iron.

7 Turn band to right side of curtain; press band, with the seamline on outer edge of curtain.

8 Pin the band in place. Stitch around the band, close to the inner fold.

9 Complete the shower curtain as for the basic curtain on page 28, steps 5 to 7.

SHOWER CURTAINS
WITH TUCKED BORDERS

In this variation of a basic shower curtain with rings, design interest is created at the lower edge. A series of three 1" (2.5 cm) tucks, spaced 1" (2.5 cm) apart, is sewn at the lower edge, with the hem edge stitched into the first tuck. When the shower curtain is made from a simple cotton fabric, the crisp tucks add a handsome border.

HOW TO SEW A SHOWER CURTAIN WITH A TUCKED BORDER

MATERIALS

- Lightweight decorator fabric.
- Twelve grommets and attaching tool, optional.
- Shower curtain liner.
- Shower curtain rod and twelve rings.

CUTTING DIRECTIONS

Cut two lengths of fabric, 16" (40.5 cm) longer than the desired finished length; for a standard 72" (183 cm) finished length, cut the fabric lengths 88" (223.5 cm) long. This allows 12" (30.5 cm) for the tucks and the hem at the lower edge and 4" (10 cm) for the hem at the upper edge. Seam the fabric widths together; if desired, stitch a French seam, as on pages 27 and 28, steps 1 to 3. Trim one side so the cut width of the shower curtain is 76" (193 cm), or 4" (10 cm) wider than the desired finished width.

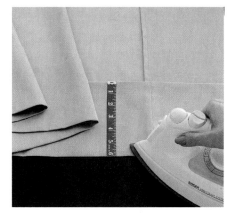

1 Seam fabric widths together. At lower edge, press under 6" (15 cm) twice to wrong side of fabric.

2 Stitch a tuck 1" (2.5 cm) from the second foldline, catching the lower edge inside the tuck. Press tuck toward lower edge of curtain panel.

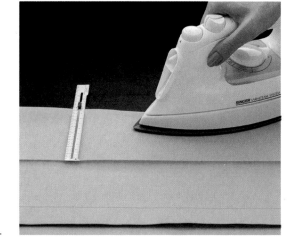

3 Press the foldline for second tuck to wrong side of the fabric, 3" (7.5 cm) above stitching line. Press foldline for third tuck to the wrong side, 4" (10 cm) above foldline for second tuck.

4 Stitch tucks 1" (2.5 cm) from foldlines. Press tucks toward lower edge of curtain panel.

5 Press under and stitch 1" (2.5 cm) double-fold hem on each side of the curtain panel.

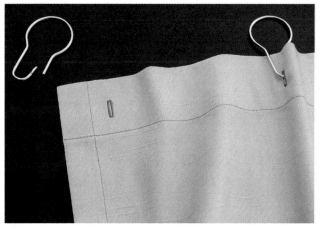

6 Complete the shower curtain as for the basic curtain on page 28, steps 5 to 7.

CURTAINS WITH DRAPED HEADINGS

A heading of matching or contrasting fabric drapes gracefully along the top of this curtain. Suitable for both shower curtains and window treatments, these curtains may be hung with sewn-on rings. Or apply buttonholes or grommets for use with hooks or snap-on rings.

When mounting the rod for a shower curtain, position the lower edge of the rod about 10" (25.5 cm) above the rod for the liner, so the liner does not show in the swooped areas between the rings. When mounting the rod for a window treatment, position the rod about 10" (25.5 cm) above the molding to keep the top of the window from showing.

Made from lightweight fabric that drapes softly, the curtain and the heading have two times fullness with the rings or hooks spaced 12" to 16" (30.5 to 40.5 cm) apart. If you prefer to use less fullness in the curtain or to space the rings closer together, the depth of the swoops will be shortened and the rod may be hung lower. Before permanently installing the rod, hang the curtain on it and hold it in place to check the height. If you are making a matching shower curtain and window treatment, you may be able to hang them both at the same height.

HOW TO SEW A CURTAIN WITH A DRAPED HEADING

MATERIALS

- Lightweight fabric that drapes softly, for the curtain; matching or contrasting lightweight, soft fabric may be used for the heading.

- Grommets and attaching tool, optional.

- Wooden pole with sew-on wooden rings, or shower bar or curtain rod with hooks or snap-on rings.

CUTTING DIRECTIONS

Determine the approximate height for mounting the shower bar or curtain rod (page 49), about 10" (25.5 cm) above the shower curtain liner or window frame.

Determine the desired finished length of the curtain by first measuring from the bottom of the rod to the floor. Subtract 2½" (6.5 cm) from this measurement, because, when hung, the curtain is about 2½" (6.5 cm) below the rod. Then subtract an amount equal to the desired clearance from the floor, usually about 2" (5 cm).

The cut length of the fabric is equal to the desired finished length of the curtain plus 3½" (9 cm). The cut width of the fabric is equal to two times the length of the rod plus 4" (10 cm); this allows for two 1" (2.5 cm) double-fold side hems. Seam the fabric widths together as necessary; if desired, stitch French seams, as on pages 27 and 28, steps 1 to 3.

For the heading, cut matching or contrasting fabric into 29" (73.5 cm) lengths. Seam the fabric widths together as necessary so the heading is equal to the hemmed width of the curtain plus 1" (2.5 cm) for seam allowances on the sides.

1 Seam fabric widths together. Press under 3" (7.5 cm) twice on lower edge of curtain panel; stitch to make 3" (7.5 cm) double-fold hem. Press under 1" (2.5 cm) twice on each side of curtain panel; stitch to make 1" (2.5 cm) double-fold side hems.

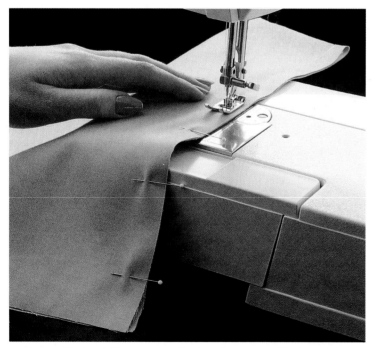

2 Seam fabric widths together for heading, using ½" (1.3 cm) conventional seams; French seams are not used. Press seams open. Fold heading in half lengthwise, right sides together; at ends, stitch ½" (1.3 cm) seams.

3 Turn the heading right side out; press the seams at ends. Baste the raw edges together; press along the fold.

4 Pin the heading to the top of the curtain panel, matching raw edges, with the right side of the heading facing down on the wrong side of the curtain panel. Stitch ½" (1.3 cm) seam; finish the seam, using zigzag or overlock stitch.

5 Fold the heading 3" (7.5 cm) above seamline as shown. Pin in place; do not press foldline.

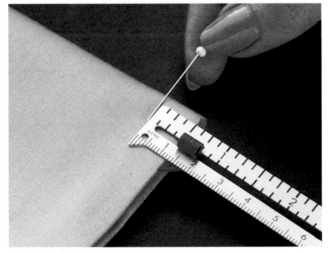

6 Mark fold at upper edge, ½" (1.3 cm) from each side of the curtain panel, to mark placement for end rings.

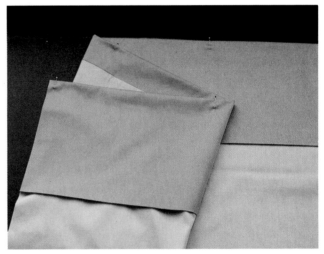

7 Mark placement for remaining rings, about 12" to 16" (30.5 to 40.5 cm) apart, dividing the distance between end marks evenly.

8 Sew rings to back side of heading at markings, using small stitches around entire metal eye **(a).** Or stitch buttonholes **(b)** or attach grommets **(c),** with the top of each buttonhole or grommet ½" (1.3 cm) below the fold at the upper edge; stitch buttonholes or attach grommets through all four layers of heading and curtain panel.

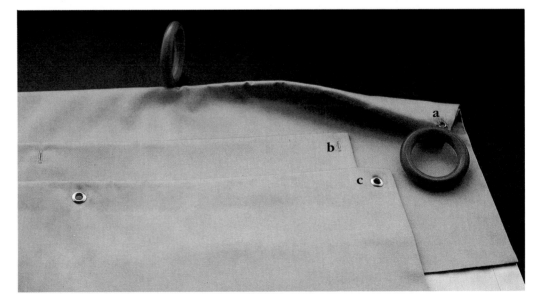

BUTTONED SWAGS

Top off a simple window treatment or shower curtain with an easy-to-sew buttoned swag valance, or use the swag over shower doors or blinds. The valance is made up of two parts: a shirred fabric sleeve that covers the rod, and a swag that buttons onto the sleeve.

The swagged fabric has one and one-half times fullness. Additional fabric is allowed for the draped fabric at the ends. The number of buttons and the distance between them varies with the width of the treatment. For a 60" (152.5 cm) shower area, it works well to use five buttons, creating four swoops; on a 36" (91.5 cm) window, use four buttons, creating just three swoops.

Choose a mediumweight decorator fabric that can support the weight of the buttoned treatment, yet drape nicely between the buttons. Because the swag is lined with self-fabric, avoid patterns that will show through the outer layer; this is especially important for window treatments, because sunlight can cause patterns to show through more noticeably.

The fabric for both the sleeve and the swag may be cut on the crosswise grain, piecing widths of fabric together to achieve the necessary size. Sometimes, the sleeve and swag may be cut on the lengthwise grain, referred to as *railroading,* to eliminate the need for seaming. Railroading can only be used for solid-colored fabrics or patterned fabrics that can be turned sideways, making it inappropriate for fabrics with one-way designs like stemmed flowers or birds. If you are using the swag with a shower curtain or window treatment, cut both the swag and the curtain on the same grainline.

The curtain rod for the swag should be mounted so the lower edge of the rod is at least 7" (18 cm) above a shower curtain rod, shower door, or window treatment, so the undertreatment does not show in the swooped areas of the swag.

HOW TO SEW A BUTTONED SWAG

MATERIALS

- Decorator fabric.
- Curtain rod, 2½" (6.5 cm) wide. For shower opening, use spring-tension rod; for a window treatment, use a wall-mounted rod with a return, or projection, deep enough to clear undertreatment.
- Decorative buttons.
- Small, flat buttons, for reinforcement on the wrong side.

CUTTING DIRECTIONS

For the rod sleeve, cut a fabric strip 7½" (19.3 cm) wide, piecing the strip as necessary to measure two and one-half to three times the length of the curtain rod. If using a wall-mount rod, the 7½" (19.3 cm) fabric strip should be two and one-half to three times the combined length of the rod and the depth of the rod return, or projection.

For the swag, cut a fabric rectangle, 33" (84 cm) wide, piecing it as necessary to measure one and one-half times the rod length plus 45" (115 cm); this allows for the swoops between the buttons and the draped fabric at the sides of the swag.

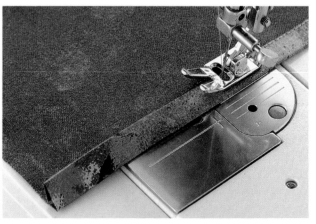

1 Press under ½" (1.3 cm) twice on the short ends of the fabric strip for the rod sleeve; stitch, to make ½" (1.3 cm) double-fold hems.

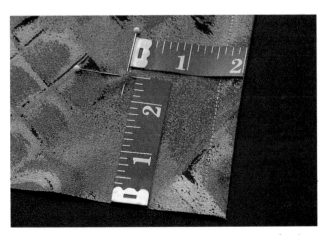

2 For a spring-tension rod. Mark a point for the button placement at each end of fabric for the sleeve, measuring 2½" (6.5 cm) from lower edge and 2" (5 cm) from hemmed edge.

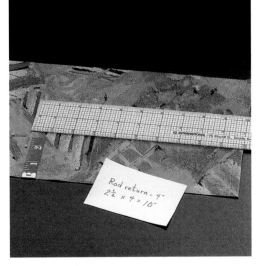

2 For a wall-mount rod. Mark a point for button placement at each end of fabric for sleeve, measuring 2½" (6.5 cm) from lower edge and measuring from each hemmed edge a distance equal to two and one-half times the depth of the rod return, or projection.

(Continued)

SHOWER & WINDOW CURTAINS

53

3 Divide the remaining length between the placement marks equally into desired number of swoops; mark the placement for the buttons, 2½" (6.5 cm) up from the lower edge.

4 Sew a button at each mark, positioning a reinforcement button on wrong side of fabric and a decorative button on right side. Sew through both of the buttons at one time; form a thread shank under the decorative button if it does not have a shank.

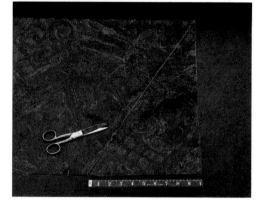

5 Fold fabric strip for sleeve in half, right sides together. Stitch ½" (1.3 cm) seam on the long edge; press seam open.

6 Turn the sleeve right side out, centering seam on back of sleeve. Buttons will be at or near lower edge.

7 Fold fabric for swag in half lengthwise, right sides together, with fold at top; pin long raw edges together at bottom. On the lower edge of swag, measure 10" (25.5 cm) from ends; mark. At each end, draw a line from mark on lower edge to end of fold at top; cut away triangular section.

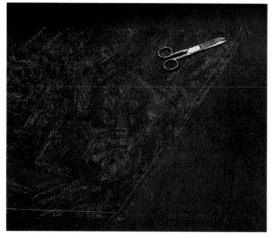

8 Sew ½" (1.3 cm) seam around the ends and lower edge of swag, leaving an opening for turning on one short end; trim corners.

9 Turn swag right side out; press. Stitch opening closed. On fold, measure 22" (56 cm) from each end of swag; mark placement for vertical buttonholes, with upper end of buttonhole ½" (1.3 cm) from the fold.

10 Divide the remaining length between marks equally into desired number of swoops; mark buttonholes. At all placement marks on swag, sew buttonholes large enough to accommodate the decorative buttons.

11 Measure a 2" (5 cm) distance below each buttonhole; fold in half as shown, making 1" (2.5 cm) tuck. Secure tucks by hand-stitching them in place, or use machine bar tacks.

HOW TO HANG A BUTTONED SWAG ON A SPRING-TENSION ROD

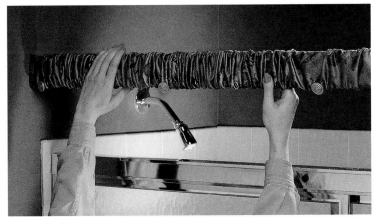

1 Slide sleeve onto spring-tension rod, with the seam centered on back of rod and the buttons at or near lower edge. Mount rod at desired height. Distribute fullness evenly so the spaces between the buttons are equal.

2 Button the swag onto shirred sleeve. Arrange the swoops between the buttons, draping the fabric as desired. Arrange the fabric at each end of the swag.

HOW TO HANG A BUTTONED SWAG ON A WALL-MOUNT ROD

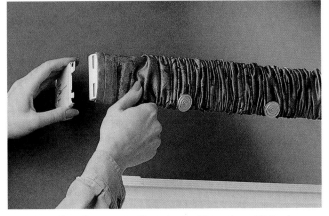

1 Mount brackets on wall at desired location. Slide sleeve onto curtain rod, with seam centered on the back of the rod and buttons about ¼" (6 mm) from the lower edge. Mount the curtain rod.

2 Slide ends of sleeve onto brackets; arrange the shirred sleeve so first and last buttons are located ½" (1.3 cm) from corners on the face of the rod. Hang and arrange the swag as in step 2, above.

MORE IDEAS FOR SHOWER CURTAINS

Contrasting fabric bands *are stitched on the tiebacks and valance at left, using the method on page 78. The bands add interest to the basic rod-pocket curtains and valance (page 31) and the tiebacks with tucked ends (page 38).*

Child's handprints *are applied to the banded shower curtain below (page 43). Dilute the fabric paint slightly with water in a shallow pan. Then dip the child's hand in the paint, and place it on the fabric, pressing down on the fingers and palm. Heat-set the fabric paint according to the manufacturer's directions.*

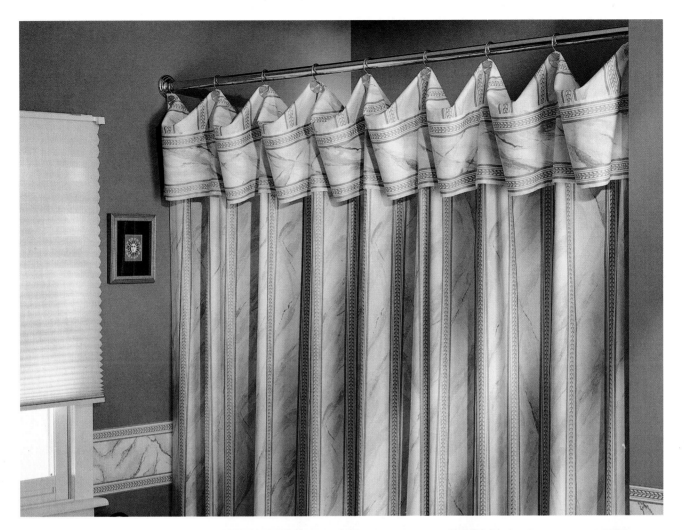

Bed sheet is used for the shower curtain above. For this curtain, use a king-size flat bed sheet, cutting 14½" (36.8 cm) from the top of the sheet to use for the draped heading (page 49). Prewash the sheet to soften it.

Wide lace edging embellishes the lower edge of the shower curtain at right. The lace is applied, adding a taffeta band along the upper edge of the lace, as on page 79.

Fabric
Accessories

SINK & VANITY SKIRTS

By adding a gathered skirt to the bathroom sink or a vanity table, you can introduce the softness of fabric into the bathroom or repeat a fabric that has been used for a window treatment or shower curtain. The sink skirt can conceal unsightly plumbing while creating a hidden storage area that is easily accessible. By attaching a skirt to a small table, you can transform it into a vanity with room for storing baskets of cosmetics and toiletries under the skirt.

For easy cleaning, make the skirt from a washable fabric and attach it to the sink or vanity table with hook and loop tape. If you will be laundering the skirt, preshrink the fabric before cutting the pieces.

Usually, sink and vanity skirts are applied to the outer surface. However, on some wall-mount sinks, a skirt can be mounted to the inner surface. Before cutting the fabric, apply the hook and loop tape to the sink and determine the finished width and length of the skirt as on page 62, steps 1 to 3.

Skirts often extend from wall to wall around the sides and front of the sink or table. However, if you intend to apply the skirt to the inner surface of a sink, you may want to extend the skirt around the back for a few inches (centimeters). If the sink or table stands away from the wall, or is round or oval in shape, you may want to apply the skirt completely around it.

MATERIALS

- Fabric.
- Sew-on hook and loop tape, ¾" (2 cm) wide, in length equal to finished width of skirt.
- Adhesive designed for use with hook and loop tape.

CUTTING DIRECTIONS

Apply the hook side of the hook and loop tape to the sink or vanity table, as on page 62, step 1; the tape may be applied for either an outside-mounted or inside-mounted skirt. Measure for the finished width and length of the skirt as on page 62, steps 2 and 3.

To determine the cut length of the fabric, add 2½" (6.5 cm) to the finished length, to allow for a 1" (2.5 cm) double-fold hem at the bottom and a ½" (1.3 cm) seam allowance at the top.

To determine the cut width, multiply the finished width of the skirt by two and one-half times fullness. Seam widths of fabric together as necessary to achieve this measurement.

Cut one 3" (7.5 cm) fabric strip for the band, with the length of the strip equal to the desired finished width of the skirt plus 1" (2.5 cm) to allow for two ½" (1.3 cm) seam allowances.

Vanity table skirt (opposite), applied to the outer surface of the apron, transforms a table into a vanity.

Sink skirt (below) adds softness to the decorating scheme of the bathroom and conceals any exposed plumbing.

TWO METHODS FOR ATTACHING A SINK OR VANITY SKIRT

Outside mount. Skirt may be attached to the outer surface of most sinks or vanity tables, using hook and loop tape.

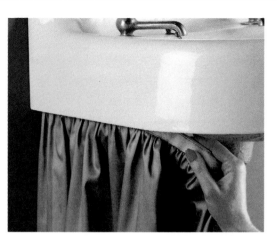

Inside mount. Skirt may be attached to the inner surface of some sinks, using hook and loop tape. On most vanity tables, the legs are positioned so an inside mount is not possible.

HOW TO MAKE A SINK OR VANITY SKIRT

1 Decide where you want the hook and loop tape, for either outside or inside mount, above; mark a placement line on the sink or table, parallel to the floor. Apply hook side of hook and loop tape to sink or table; affix tape with adhesive designed for the hook and loop tape, according to the manufacturer's directions.

2 Secure loop side of hook and loop tape over the hook side. Determine finished width of skirt by measuring around sink or vanity where skirt will be attached; measure over the tape on inside or outside.

3 Measure for the finished length of the skirt, from the lower edge of the tape to the floor; subtract ½" (1.3 cm) from this measurement, to allow for clearance at the floor. Cut the fabric (page 61).

4 Press under 1" (2.5 cm) twice on the lower edge of skirt; stitch to make 1" (2.5 cm) double-fold hem. Press under and stitch ½" (1.3 cm) double-fold hems on sides of skirt.

5 Zigzag over a cord at the upper edge of the skirt, within seam allowance, just beyond seamline.

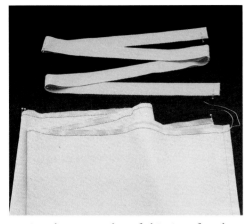

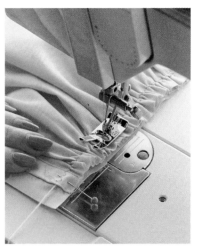

6 Divide upper edge of skirt into fourths; pin-mark. Press band in half lengthwise, matching the long edges. Pin-mark one long edge of the band ½" (1.3 cm) from each end; divide the distance between pins into fourths, and pin-mark. Unfold band.

7 Pin skirt to the band, right sides together, matching pin marks. Pull up gathering cord, and gather skirt evenly to fit. Pin in place.

8 Stitch the band to the skirt in ½" (1.3 cm) seam. Press seam allowances toward the band.

9 Position loop side of hook and loop tape on band, ⅛" (3 mm) from pressed line; place the tape on back of band if the skirt will be applied to outside surface of sink or table **(a),** or place on front of band if the skirt will be applied to inside surface **(b).** Stitch along both long edges of tape.

10 Press under ⅜" (1 cm) on remaining long edge of band. Fold band, right sides together, along pressed center line. Stitch ½" (1.3 cm) seams at ends; trim.

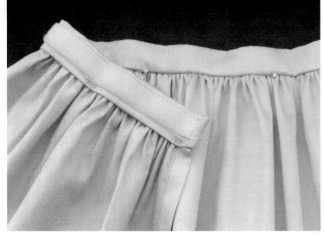

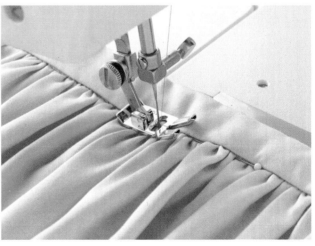

11 Turn band right side out, enclosing seam allowances; press ends. From the right side of skirt, pin the band in place along seamline, catching the lower edge of band on wrong side.

12 Stitch in the ditch from the right side by stitching in the well of the seam. Attach skirt, using an outside or inside mount, as shown opposite.

FRINGED RUGS

Fringed rugs with a thick, plush nap make comfortable bath mats and add textural interest to the bathroom. To create this look, strips of fabric are sewn to a backing, then cut into fringe. The rug is machine washed and machine dried several times, until the cut edges curl and fray.

Select washable lightweight to mediumweight fabrics, such as broadcloth or cotton sheeting. Fabrics that are 100 percent cotton are the most absorbent and give a rich textural effect, because, when washed, they curl, fray, and wrinkle significantly. Cotton/polyester blends may be used with 100 percent cottons to provide more variation in the rug's texture, but cotton blends do not curl and fray as well. Fabrics of 100 percent rayon are likely to ravel too much, and knit fabrics generally do not curl or fray at all.

You may want to make a small test sample of the rug, to decide on the fabrics to use and the relative amounts of each fabric. For a varied effect, you may want to try a combination of smooth-surfaced broadcloths with seersuckers. Or mix yarn-dyed plaids, stripes, and checks with solid-colored fabrics. Keep in mind that the wrong side of a printed fabric may show, which may not be desirable.

Cotton canvas or cotton drill, most readily available in white or off-white, is used for the backing fabric. In most cases, the cut fringe covers the backing. If the fringe fabrics are light-colored, it is not objectionable to see a white backing fabric, should the fringe not completely cover it. If the fringe fabrics are dark or bright in color and a coordinating canvas backing is unavailable, you may want to layer a coordinating fabric over the backing before you start sewing the fringe strips in place.

The beauty of this rug is in the wrinkling and curling of the fringe after it is machine washed and dried. Unless you are using fabrics with special care instructions, the rug is laundered with detergent, using the normal cycle of the machine. When machine drying, place an old terry cloth towel in the dryer with the rug, to help separate the layers of the cut fringe and fluff the rug.

The final appearance of this rug depends primarily on its fabric colors and fiber content. Considerations such as quality, straight grain, and precise cutting and sewing will have minimal effect on the final results. Therefore, the rug can be cut and sewn without a lot of fuss.

Use the worksheet on page 66 to calculate the total number of fabric strips you need for the rug. Then decide how many of these strips you want to cut from each fabric. You may want an even amount of each fabric. Or you may want to cut more strips from some of the fabrics, to make them more predominant.

As you would with any rug that does not have a nonslip backing, place a purchased nonslip pad between the rug and the floor.

Oval rug (opposite) combines several colors of hand-dyed fabric in 100 percent cotton.

Rectangular rug (right) has assorted plaids and solids with a subtle color variation. Some fabrics are 100 percent cotton and some are cotton blends.

WORKSHEET FOR CALCULATING THE FABRIC FOR THE FRINGE

Desired finished width of rug in inches (cm)	=
Multiplied by 2	×
Number of inner rows	=
Plus two outer rows	+
Total number of rows	=
Multiplied by desired finished length of rug in inches (cm)	×
Total linial length of rows for rectangular or square rug	=
Plus distance around perimeter of rug, if making oval or round rug	+
Total lineal length of rows for oval or round rug	=
Total lineal length of rows (as determined above for rectangular or square rug, or oval or round rug) divided by fabric width, not including selvages	÷
Total number of strips to cut (round up to next whole number)*	=
Multiply by width of strip, or 5" (12.5 cm)	×
Fabric required in inches (cm)	=

If more than one fabric is used for the rug, decide how many strips you want from each fabric. To determine the amount of each fabric needed, complete the worksheet by multiplying the number of strips for each fabric by 5" (12.5 cm).

MATERIALS

- Lightweight to mediumweight cotton or cotton-blend fabrics, for the cut fringe.
- Heavy cotton canvas or drill, for the backing.
- Fabric to cover the backing, optional.
- Nonslip pad, to place under the finished rug.

CUTTING DIRECTIONS

For a rectangular or square rug, cut the canvas or drill backing 1½" (3.8 cm) longer and wider than the desired finished size of the rug, to allow for ¾" (2 cm) hem allowances. For an oval or round rug, cut the canvas or drill backing to the finished size; the edges are not hemmed. Cut fabric to cover the backing, if desired, to the same size as the backing.

For the fringe, trim the selvages from the fabrics. Cut 5" (12.5 cm) fabric strips across the width of the fabric; refer to the worksheet at left for the approximate number of fabric strips needed.

HOW TO MAKE A RECTANGULAR OR SQUARE FRINGED RUG

1 Pin layer of fabric on the backing, if necessary (page 65). Finish the raw edges of the backing. Press ¾" (2 cm) hem allowances to wrong side; stitch in place.

2 Draw lengthwise placement lines on the right side of the backing, ½" (1.3 cm) apart.

3 Press fabric strips in half lengthwise, matching the raw edges.

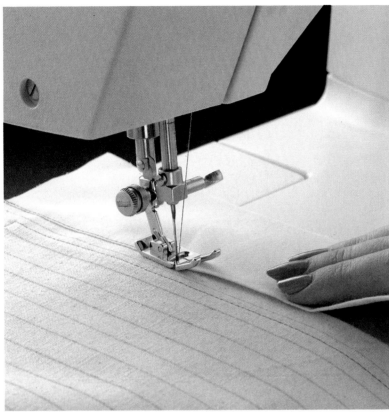

4 Stitch first fabric strip to the backing, with folded edge of strip just covering one long edge of the backing and with raw edges extending out from backing.

5 Trim off excess fabric strip at end, even with edge of backing.

6 Stitch next fabric strip to backing, with the folded edge on the first placement line and with strip facing in same direction as first row. At end, trim the strip even with edge of backing.

7 Repeat step 6 for subsequent rows. To add another strip within a row, butt end of new strip to previous strip, and continue stitching.

(Continued)

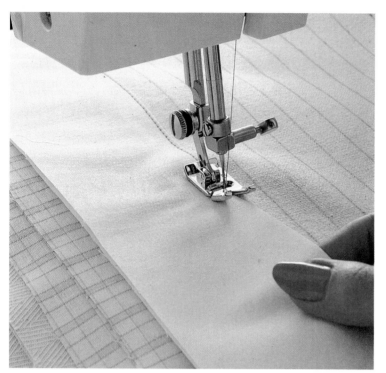

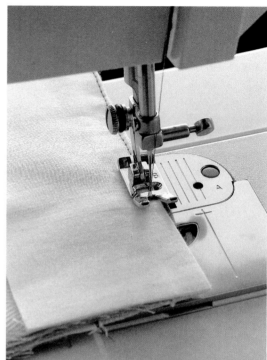

8 Rotate rug in opposite direction when about one-half of the rows are completed, to eliminate bulk of fabric under the head of the sewing machine. Stitch remaining rows, with strips facing in same direction as first half of rows.

9 Stitch last fabric strip with folded edge even with hemmed edge of backing.

11 Machine wash and machine dry rug several times, to achieve frayed and curled look.

10 Cut the fabric strips through both layers at ½" (1.3 cm) intervals, cutting up to ½" (1.3 cm) from fold. When cutting, fold all remaining fabric out of the way and place a straightedge under the strip you are cutting.

HOW TO MAKE AN OVAL OR ROUND FRINGED RUG

1 Pin a layer of fabric on the backing, if necessary (page 65). Finish raw edges.

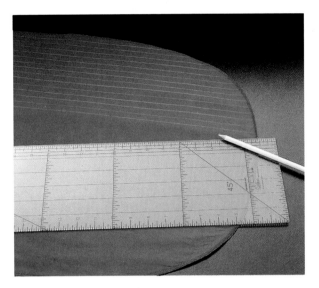

2 Mark placement lines on right side of backing, along straight of grain, ½" (1.3 cm) apart; on an oval rug, mark the lines lengthwise. Press fabric strips as on page 66, step 3.

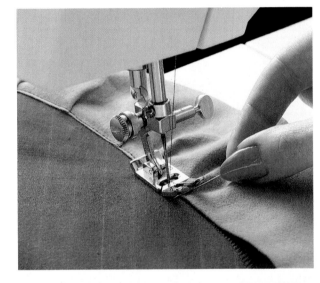

3 Stitch first fabric strip around backing, with the folded edge of the strip overlapping the edge of backing ¼" (6 mm) and with raw edges extending out from backing. Ease strip to backing as you sew, by pushing small tucks in strip with pin; do not stitch over pins.

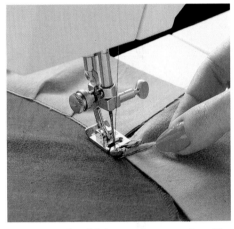

4 Butt ends of fabric strips together if more than one strip is needed, and butt strips at beginning and end of circle.

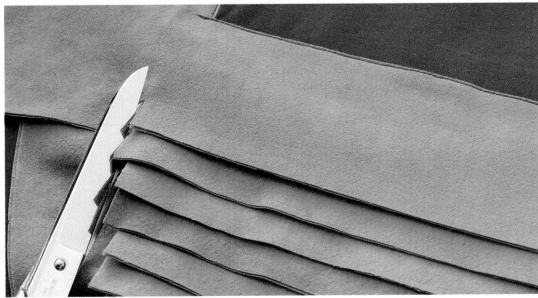

5 Stitch the remaining rows as on pages 67 and 68, steps 6 to 8, except trim fabric strips at ends so they overlap the outer fabric strip ¼" (6 mm). Complete rug as in steps 10 and 11, opposite.

BRAIDED RUGS FROM SWEATSHIRT FLEECE

Hand-braided oval rugs, traditionally constructed from strips of wool, can be made from strips of sweatshirt fleece for a soft, warm bathroom rug that is easily laundered.

Sweatshirt fleece with a high-cotton fiber content is most desirable because of its absorbancy and body, although blends of other fiber contents may be used. Because the fabric is cut into strips and braided, it is not important to use high-quality fabrics. Remnants and flawed fabrics may be used to make the project even more affordable. As a general guideline, ¾ yd. (0.7 m) fabric is needed for 1 sq. ft. (0.32 sq. m). Three 2" (5 cm) strips of 60" (152.5 cm) sweatshirt fleece make a braid about 42" (107 cm) long. To prevent the rug from shrinking, launder the fabrics before beginning the project.

After the fabric strips are braided, the braid is coiled into rows and the rows are laced together. For the lacing, use cotton carpet thread, threaded on a lacer. If a lacer is not available, a large-eyed craft needle with a blunt or rounded end can be used. The lacer or needle is pushed through the loops of the braid and should not pierce the fabric.

For easier handling, you can alternate the braiding and lacing. You may want to braid until the first three fabric strips are almost used up. Then clamp the braid and begin the lacing, continuing up to the clamp. Join new strips, and resume braiding. Repeat this process until the rug is completed.

Braided rugs are reversible and look almost the same from both sides. For clarity, however, the instructions that follow refer to the front and back sides; braiding is done from the front of the rug and lacing the braids together, from the back.

MATERIALS

- Sweatshirt fleece; one, two, or three colors may be used to make the braid.
- Rotary cutter and mat.
- Heavy carpet thread.
- Lacer, such as Braidkin™, or a large-eyed craft needle with blunt or rounded end.
- Clamp, for holding fabric strips during braiding.
- Clothespins or other small clamps, to secure ends of braid during lacing.
- Hand-sewing needle and thread.
- Nonslip pad, to place under the finished rug.

HOW TO MAKE A BRAIDED RUG FROM SWEATSHIRT FLEECE

1 Cut sweatshirt fleece into 2" (5 cm) strips across the width of fabric. Join two fabric strips, fleece sides together, stitching on the bias by hand or machine. Trim seam allowances to ¼" (6 mm). Finger-press seam open.

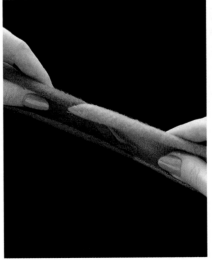

2 Fold the raw edges to the center, stretching the strip slightly so the edges roll inward.

3 Fold edges of third strip to center; fold in half with open side to the right. Insert strip between layers of joined strips from step 1, at seam; fold joined strips in half, enclosing end of third strip. Stitch in place.

(Continued)

HOW TO MAKE A BRAIDED RUG FROM SWEATSHIRT FLEECE
(CONTINUED)

4 Clamp the joined strips to work surface. To begin braiding, place left strip over center strip, then right strip over center strip; keep the strips folded with open side to the right.

5 Continue braiding as in step 4 until length of braid equals the desired finished length of rug minus the desired finished width. Maintain even tension while braiding.

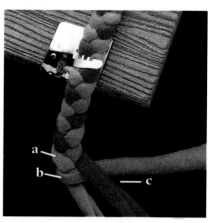

6 Place left strip (a) over center strip, then left strip (b) over center strip again. Next, place right strip (c) over center strip, and pull tightly.

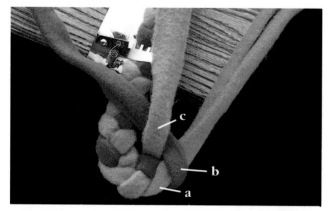

7 Repeat sequence in step 6 again, as indicated by a, b, and c. The braid curls around as you braid, forming a tight curve.

8 Braid strips as in step 4, up to about 6" (15 cm) from ends. Clamp strips with clothespin.

9 Lay braid on a flat surface, with back side up, turning braid back against itself where it curves. Secure lacing thread to center loop on the inner turn of the braid.

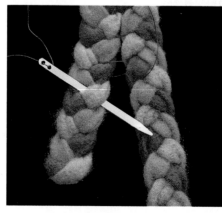

10 Lace braid together by pushing the lacer into loop on one side, then into loop on opposite side; continue by lacing every loop and alternating sides, up to end where you started braiding.

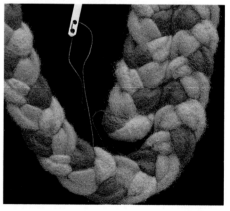

11 Push the lacer through end loop of rug, then push lacer through loop on braid, skipping one loop. Repeat. By skipping a loop on the braid, you are "increasing"; this allows rug to lie flat on floor without cupping.

12 Lace rug without increasing on straight sides of the rug. Increase around curved ends as necessary for rug to lie flat. When the thread is inside a loop on rug, if the next loop on the braid is even with or behind the thread **(a),** skip it and lace the next loop **(b).** Keep rug flat on surface as you lace.

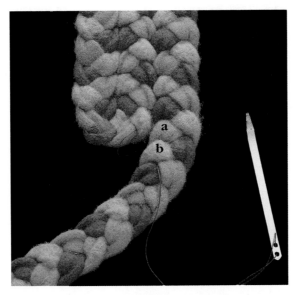

13 Join new strips to ends of braided strips as necessary, as in step 1.

14 Continue braiding and lacing until the desired size is achieved, increasing as necessary so rug lies flat; keep an even tension while braiding. Join new thread to lacing thread, whenever it is necessary, by tying a strong knot; then hide the ends under a loop of rug.

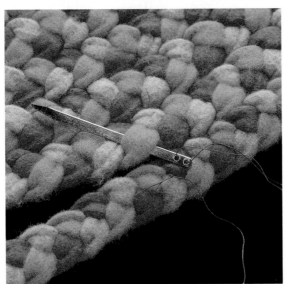

15 Finish the rug by ending the braid on a curve, tapering the last 6" to 8" (15 to 20.5 cm) by trimming strips up to one-half the original width. Refold strips.

16 Braid to the ends of the strips; hand-stitch ends together.

17 Lace rug as far as possible; then back-lace for 3" to 4" (7.5 to 10 cm). Secure lacing thread with a knot before cutting.

18 Tuck end into closest loop; hand-stitch in place with a needle and thread.

Satin binding and appliqués add an elegant touch to the terry towels above. The appliqué is stitched using the reverse appliqué technique (page 76). The scalloped edge is bound with a bias polyester satin (page 77).

Fabric bands (page 78) provide simple detailing on terry towels.

Overlocked edge finish (page 79) accents the fan-folded towel at left, and a purchased fusible monogram adds a personalized touch. Simply iron the monogram in place, and brush the towel lightly to raise the flattened nap.

DECORATIVE TOWELS

Lace trim (page 79) may be added as an edging along the lower edge of a towel or as a band across the width, as shown on the towels above.

Create your own specialty bath towels at a fraction of the cost of purchased towels sold in bath shops. To add fine detailing to towels, trim them with appliqués, fabric bands, bindings, and lace trims. Or use purchased monograms to personalize your towels, and add a decorative edge finish, using a serger.

For embellishing towels, select mediumweight washable fabrics. Polyester taffetas and satins are good choices, because they have a subtle sheen, hold their shape as they are being applied to terry cloth, and launder well. Taffeta and satin also make decorative appliqués; for best results on terry cloth, use the reverse appliqué method and simple appliqué designs. For another look, bands of color can be added to towels in single or multiple rows, using bias strips of polyester taffeta or satin.

Bias strips of polyester taffeta or satin also work well for binding a scalloped edge on the lower edge of a towel. For easier sewing, the scallops should be gently curved with no more than 1" (2.5 cm) depth from the lowest to the highest point on the curve. Plan a symmetrical design that has an odd number of scallops so the design begins and ends at the same distance from the lower edge of the towel.

Lace trims may appear delicate, but cotton, nylon, and polyester laces are actually quite durable. Popular choices for embellishing towels include eyelet, Schiffli, and Cluny laces. Use galloon lace, which has scalloped, finished edges on both sides, for a band near the bottom of the towel. Or use lace edging to conceal the fringe or hem at the lower edge, stitching a bias strip of polyester taffeta at the top of the lace edging.

An overlocked edge finish, sewn on a serger, defines the edge of a towel with contrasting stitches. This technique is most successful when you stitch along the selvages of the towel without trimming the edge with the blades of the serger. Especially attractive for towels displayed in a fan fold, the decorative overlock stitches emphasize the fanned edge.

HOW TO EMBELLISH A TOWEL WITH REVERSE APPLIQUÉ

MATERIALS

- Purchased plain towel.
- Washable mediumweight fabrics, such as polyester satin or taffeta, for the appliqué.
- Tear-away stabilizer.
- Cotton machine embroidery thread in colors to match appliqué fabrics; regular thread to match towel.

1 Trace the mirror image of appliqué design onto tear-away stabilizer. Number sections of design in the sequence they will be applied, beginning with those that should appear to be under other pieces. Cut the stabilizer at least 2" (5 cm) larger than the entire design.

2 Position tear-away stabilizer on wrong side of towel in the desired location. Baste in place.

3 Cut the fabric for first piece to be applied, leaving ample margin around the shape. Pin in place, right side up, on right side of towel; insert pins from wrong side of towel, through stabilizer.

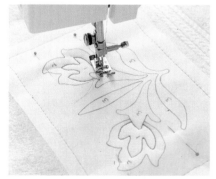

4 Stitch on design line for first shape, using short, straight stitches; use thread that matches towel.

5 Remove the pins. Trim the excess appliqué fabric close to stitching from right side, taking care not to cut loops or pile of towel.

6 Repeat steps 3 to 5 for each piece in the appliqué, applying pieces in sequence as numbered in step 1.

7 Set the machine for closely spaced zigzag stitches; set the stitch width as desired. Loosen needle thread tension, if necessary, so the bobbin thread will not show on right side. Using thread that matches towel in the bobbin and thread that matches appliqué in needle, satin stitch on design lines from right side; stitch sections in numbered sequence.

8 Remove tear-away stabilizer from wrong side of towel, taking care not to pull loops or pile of towel.

HOW TO SCALLOP & BIND A TOWEL EDGE

MATERIALS

- Purchased plain towel.

- Washable mediumweight fabric, such as polyester satin or taffeta, for the binding.

1 Make a pattern for the scalloped edge on tissue paper; plan for an odd number of gently curved scallops, with the depth of the scallops from the lowest to the highest point no more than 1" (2.5 cm). Pin pattern to towel in the desired location. Cut scalloped edge.

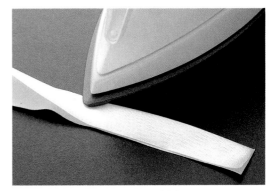

2 Cut 2" (5 cm) bias strip of fabric; piece strips together, if necessary, to make binding strip. Press strip in half lengthwise, wrong sides together, taking care not to distort width of the strip.

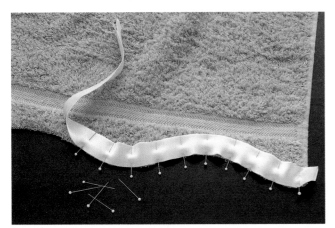

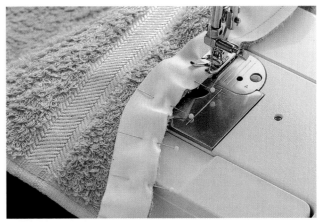

3 Pin binding strip to right side of towel, along scalloped edge, with the raw edges even; extend the binding ½" (1.3 cm) beyond sides of towel.

4 Stitch a scant ¼" (6 mm) from raw edges, easing the binding strip to fit curves of scallop.

5 Press the binding strip lightly toward lower edge. Fold ends of binding over the sides of towel; press. Wrap binding around the scalloped edge, and pin in the ditch of the seam.

6 Stitch in the ditch on the right side of the towel, catching binding on the wrong side of the towel.

HOW TO ADD A FABRIC BAND TO A TOWEL

MATERIALS

• Purchased plain towel.

• Washable mediumweight fabric, such as polyester satin or taffeta, for the band.

$3 \times 1" - 1/8" = 2\frac{7}{8}"$

1 Cut a bias strip of the fabric, with cut width of strip ⅛" (3 mm) narrower than three times the desired finished width; cut the strip 1" (2.5 cm) longer than the width of towel.

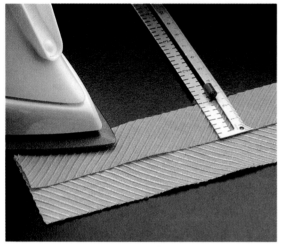

2 Place fabric strip right side down on ironing surface. Press up an amount equal to desired finished width of band, taking care not to distort or stretch the fabric.

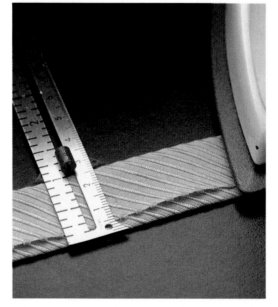

3 Press up opposite edge of fabric strip, so width between the pressed edges is equal to the finished width of the band, taking care not to distort fabric. On upper layer, raw edge does not meet the pressed edge.

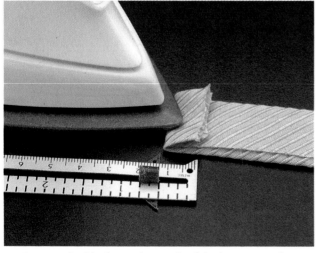

4 Press under ½" (1.3 cm) at ends of the bias strip, taking care not to distort or stretch fabric.

5 Pin bias fabric strip to towel in desired location. Stitch along outer edges of folded strip, stitching in the same direction on both sides; stitch ends.

HOW TO APPLY LACE TRIM TO A TOWEL

MATERIALS

- Purchased plain towel.
- Galloon lace or lace edging.

- Washable mediumweight fabric, such as polyester satin or taffeta, if fabric band is desired.

1 **Galloon lace.** Cut lace 1" (2.5 cm) longer than width of towel. Turn under ½" (1.3 cm) at ends; pin lace in place at the desired distance above lower edge of towel.

2 Stitch along folded ends and both scalloped edges of the lace, using straight stitch.

Lace edging. Follow step 1, left, except pin lace so it covers lower edge of towel. Stitch along folded ends and upper edge of lace, using straight stitch. If upper edge of lace is unfinished or additional detailing is desired, cover the upper edge with a bias fabric band (opposite).

HOW TO STITCH AN OVERLOCKED EDGE FINISH ON A TOWEL

MATERIALS

- Purchased plain towel.
- Tapestry needle.

- Woolly nylon thread and regular thread in contrasting color.

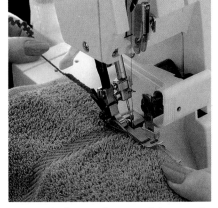

1 Set serger for balanced 3-thread overlock stitch, threading both loopers with woolly nylon thread; use regular thread in needle. Set stitch width at 4 to 5 mm; set stitch length at 1 mm.

2 Stitch along selvages of the towel, holding the tail chain taut as you begin stitching; avoid trimming edge of the towel with serger blade. Leave long tail chain at ends.

3 Thread tail chain through eye of tapestry needle, and weave the needle under overlock stitches for about 1" (2.5 cm); cut off remaining length of the tail chain.

DISPLAYING TOWELS

Rolled towels (right), neatly tucked into the compartments of a wine rack, form a colorful display.

Basketful of rolled towels (below) is placed conveniently near the shower.

Rolled-and-tied towel is set out for an overnight guest. A bar of scented soap is tucked under the pretty bow.

Fan-folded towels are displayed in a country-style galvanized pot. The edges of the towels are overlocked, using a serger as on page 79.

Towel ring is used to hang a towel, jabot-style. To fold the towel, hold it by one of the corners, allowing it to hang diagonally. Starting with the shortest corner in front, accordion-fold the towel with your other hand.

More
Accessories

CREATIVE TOWEL BARS, RINGS & HOOKS

Because the selection of purchased towel bars and rings is somewhat limited, you may prefer to decorate the bathroom with more creative hardware. Several types of hardware designed for curtains and draperies are also suitable as towel holders, making it possible to coordinate the hardware for hanging the towels with that of the window treatment. Shown here are several examples, including wooden poles, iron curtain rods, holdbacks, and swag holders.

Besides drapery hardware, other items can also be used for towel holders. For a whimsical approach, choose from the creative ideas on pages 86 and 87. For some items, it may be necessary to protect the finish from moisture by painting it or applying a clear acrylic finish.

Medallion-style holdbacks *are a creative alternative* *to towel rings.*

Iron curtain rods, available in any size, are used with your choice of iron finials for a custom towel bar.

Swag holders *can be used instead of towel rings. Matching hardware may be used for a swagged window treatment.*

Iron tieback holders *(right) are hung vertically to hold bath towels.*

Decorative wood pole sets *make a dramatic statement. The poles can be cut to any length.*

(Continued)

CREATIVE TOWEL BARS, RINGS & HOOKS (CONTINUED)

Small shovel *is hung between two cafe brackets.*

Baseball bat *(left) becomes a creative towel bar in a child's bathroom. The wood is protected with a clear acrylic finish, and the bat is secured to banister brackets.*

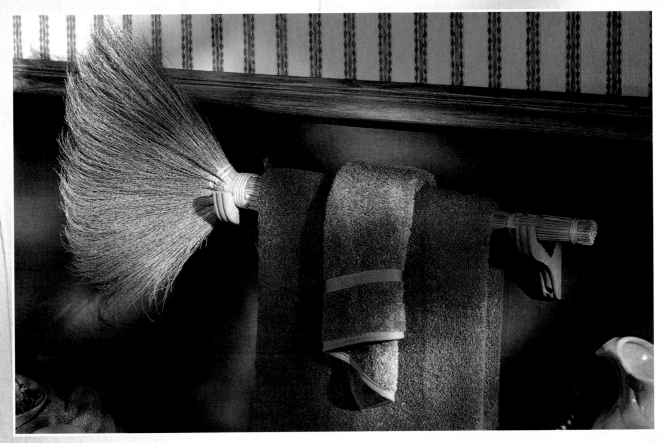

Straw broom is hung between wooden brackets designed to hang the pole for a window treatment. Nail the broom handle to the brackets to hold it in place.

Mailbox with magazine hooks is used for holding magazines as well as towels.

Shaker peg rail is a handy addition. The rail is painted and then finished with clear acrylic, to protect the wood.

FRAMED MIRRORS

Create a focal point in the bathroom by using a beautiful picture frame as the frame for a wall mirror. A smaller picture frame can be used as a tabletop vanity mirror, to display perfume bottles or a grouping of votive candles.

Be sure the *rabbet,* the recess on the inner edge of the picture frame, can accommodate a ⅛" or ¼" (3 or 6 mm) mirror plus a ⅛" or ¼" (3 or 6 mm) hardboard backing. Keep in mind that ⅛" (3 mm) mirrors weigh 1½ lb. (750 g) per sq. ft. (0.32 sq. m) and ¼" (6 mm) mirrors weigh 3¼ lb. (1.6 kg) per sq. ft. (0.32 sq. m); the ⅛" (3 mm) thickness works well without causing distortion in the mirrored image, except in very large mirrors. Custom-size mirrors are available from glass companies and specialty mirror stores. Have the mirror cut to the length and width that fits within the rabbet.

After placing the mirror and the hardboard backing into the rabbet, hold the mirror in place by nailing brads into the frame as if mounting a picture. To hang the framed mirror on the wall, secure two swivel hangers onto the back of the frame. Then hook the swivel hangers onto picture hangers or mirror hangers, mounted on the wall. Select picture hangers or mirror hangers that will support the weight of the mirror; weight limitations are specified on the package.

Picture frames may be used to frame wall or tray mirrors, for a custom look and size. The vanity tray above uses a picture frame embellished with beads.

HOW TO MOUNT A FRAMED MIRROR

MATERIALS

- Picture frame.
- Mirror, cut to fit within rabbet of picture frame; thickness of mirror may be ⅛" or ¼" (3 or 6 mm), depending on depth of rabbet.
- ⅛" or ¼" (3 or 6 mm) hardboard, for backing.
- Corner braces and screws, to strengthen mitered corners of mirror; screws must be shorter than thickness of mirror frame, to prevent puncturing front of frame.
- Double-stick framer's tape and brown craft paper, for dust cover on the back of the mirror frame.
- ¾" (2 cm) brads; framer's fitting tool or split-joint pliers.
- Two swivel hangers and screws, to mount onto the back of the mirror frame.
- Two picture hangers or mirror hangers and screws, to mount onto wall; select hangers that will support the weight of the mirror.
- Jigsaw; awl; mat knife.

1 Place the picture frame facedown. Secure corner braces across mitered corners of the frame, using an awl to puncture pilot holes for screws into frame as shown; then screw braces to the frame.

2 Cut backing board from hardboard to same size as the mirror; wipe clean. Set the mirror facedown into rabbet of the picture frame; then place hardboard over mirror, within rabbet.

3 Insert ¾" (2 cm) brads into the middle of each side of frame, using a framer's fitting tool **(a)**. Or use split-joint pliers **(b)**, protecting the outer edge of the molding with a strip of cardboard.

4 Insert brads along each side, about 1" (2.5 cm) from the corners and at 2" (5 cm) intervals.

5 Attach double-stick framer's tape to back of frame, about ⅛" (3 mm) from outer edges. Remove paper covering.

6 Cut brown craft paper 2" (5 cm) larger than frame. Place paper on the back of the frame; stretch paper taut at center of each side, creasing it over outer edge of frame and securing it to tape.

7 Stretch paper and secure it to the tape, working from the center out to each corner; crease paper over outer edge of frame.

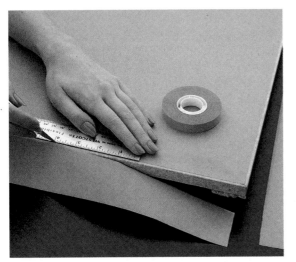

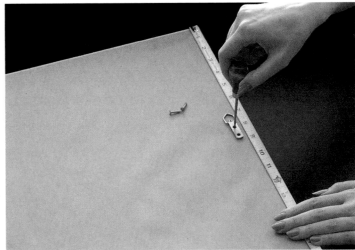

8 Trim the paper about ⅛" (3 mm) inside the creased line, using mat knife.

9 Mark the placement for swivel hangers on sides of frame, about one-third of the way down from the top. Centerpunch frame with an awl, and attach swivel hangers with screws.

10 Measure and mark placement for mirror or picture hangers on wall, so hangers will be spaced same distance apart as swivel hangers on frame; use a carpenter's level to evenly mark lines horizontally. Secure mirror or picture hangers at the markings. Hang the mirror.

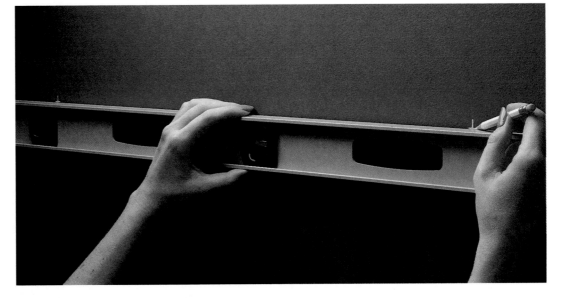

DECORATIVE WASTEBASKETS

Wastebaskets *may be covered with fabric or decorative papers. On this page, a variety of wastebaskets includes one covered in a contemporary fabric, one with torn handmade papers, and one with floral cutouts from greeting cards.*

Customize a plastic or metal wastebasket by using a variety of papers to make a decoupage wastebasket. Or make one with a removable fabric cover that coordinates with the decorating scheme of the bathroom.

For a decoupage wastebasket, choose from a variety of suitable papers. For a contemporary look, try tissue papers, cut and applied randomly. For a romantic look, select gift-wrapping papers in floral patterns. Or for an Old World look, use old newspapers, postcards, or maps. After the decoupage is completed, give the wastebasket a protective, washable finish by applying two or three coats of clear acrylic finish.

For a fabric-covered wastebasket, select a round or oval wastebasket with straight sides and no upper lip. The top of the wastebasket may be larger than the bottom, provided the sides are not curved.

For the removable cover, use mediumweight washable fabrics for the outer fabric and lining. Before sewing the cover, launder the fabrics to preshrink them. Purchased welting may be used at the top of the fabric cover, or you may make your own welting, using matching or contrasting fabric. The fabric cover is held in place with pieces of hook and loop tape at the top of the wastebasket.

HOW TO MAKE A REMOVABLE FABRIC COVER FOR A WASTEBASKET

MATERIALS

- Washable mediumweight fabrics, for the outer fabric and lining.
- Purchased welting or cording and fabric to make your own welting.
- Two circles of self-adhesive hook and loop tape, if necessary to secure the cover at top of a wastebasket with sloping sides.

CUTTING DIRECTIONS

From outer fabric, cut a rectangle about 6" (15 cm) longer than the height of the wastebasket and about 6" (15 cm) wider than the upper circumference; follow steps 1 and 2, below, for cutting the upper cover from the rectangle. Follow step 3 to cut the fabric for the bottom of the wastebasket. Cut the lining pieces for the upper cover and the bottom, using the outer fabric pieces as the pattern.

If you are making your own welting, cut a bias strip from fabric, 1" (2.5 cm) wider than the circumference of the cording and 2" (5 cm) longer than the upper edge of the cover. If you are using purchased welting, cut the welting 2" (5 cm) longer than the upper edge of the fabric cover and trim the seam allowances of the welting ½" (1.3 cm) from the stitching.

1 Place wastebasket squarely on the right side of the fabric rectangle. Wrap the fabric snugly around the wastebasket; pin in place in a straight line, up the back of the wastebasket. Use a pencil to mark the pinned seamline; also mark the upper and lower edges of the wastebasket.

2 Remove the pins. Add ⅝" (1.5 cm) seam allowances to upper edge and sides. Add ½" (1.3 cm) seam allowance to lower edge.

3 Trace around bottom of the wastebasket on wrong side of fabric, using a pencil. Add ½" (1.3 cm) seam allowance. Cut the lining pieces, above.

4 Fold upper cover piece from the outer fabric, right sides together; stitch a ½" (1.3 cm) back seam, and press open. Repeat for lining.

(Continued)

5 Make the welting, if desired, by folding fabric strip around cording, wrong sides together, matching raw edges. Using a zipper foot, machine-baste close to the cording.

6 Stitch the welting to right side of upper cover at upper edge, matching raw edges and starting 2" (5 cm) from end of welting.

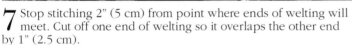

7 Stop stitching 2" (5 cm) from point where ends of welting will meet. Cut off one end of welting so it overlaps the other end by 1" (2.5 cm).

8 Remove stitching from one end of welting, and trim ends of cording so they just meet.

9 Fold under ½" (1.3 cm) of fabric on overlapping end. Lap it around the other end; finish stitching welting to upper edge.

10 Slip lining over the upper cover, right sides together, matching seams and raw edges. On upper edge, stitch ½" (1.3 cm) seam, crowding cording. Trim seam allowances.

11 Turn cover right side out. Baste lower edges of upper cover and lining together a scant ½" (1.3 cm) from edge. Clip to stitching every ½" (1.3 cm). Pin-mark lower edge into fourths.

12 Divide the outer edge of the bottom piece into fourths, and pin-mark. Pin upper cover to bottom, right sides together, matching pin marks. Stitch ½" (1.3 cm) seam.

13 Slide the cover onto the wastebasket, smoothing it in place; welting rests just above upper edge of wastebasket. If necessary, hold cover in place, using two sets of hook and loop tape circles on opposite sides of the wastebasket, near the top.

HOW TO MAKE A DECOUPAGE WASTEBASKET

MATERIALS

- Wastebasket.
- Desired selection of papers.
- Decoupage medium.
- Two paintbrushes, one for applying decoupage medium and one for dry-brushing papers in place.
- Clear acrylic finish; sponge applicator.

1 Plan design, and cut or tear papers into desired shapes and sizes. For random designs, papers may be cut or torn as they are applied. Avoid using large pieces that do not conform to shape of the wastebasket, because they would wrinkle.

3 Wrap paper around upper edge; apply narrow strip of paper to inside top. Allow decoupage medium to dry thoroughly. Apply two or three coats of clear acrylic finish, using a sponge applicator; allow finish to dry between coats.

2 Apply even layer of decoupage medium to the wrong side of paper, using slightly moist paintbrush; then apply paper to the wastebasket, using dry paintbrush to smooth in place. Continue applying papers to entire wastebasket.

POTPOURRI

Potpourri makes a decorative room accent, and it emits a delicate aroma in the bathroom. Although several premixed types of potpourri are available, you may prefer to mix your own. You can create a potpourri with the fragrance, look, and colors that suit you best, using your favorite assortment of materials.

Select from the four potpourri blends that follow, varying the ingredients to your liking, if desired. For a woodsy fragrance and look, choose the pine-forest blend, or, for a countryside aroma, choose the mix of wildflowers and herbs. For a more delicate scent, try either the citrus or the rose blend.

In each of these blends, the dominant scented and decorative materials, including flower heads and petals, wood, bark, or fruit, set the theme of the potpourri. In addition to the dominant materials, herbs and spices also contribute to the overall fragrance. Scented herbs, such as rosemary, mint, and thyme, add interest to the dominant scent, providing more complexity. Spices contribute richness, depth, and, sometimes, a piquant note.

Essential oils are added to the potpourri, to enhance the scents of the plant materials while adding fragrance of their own. If the plant materials do not have strong scents, the essential oils actually dictate the perfume of the potpourri. Essential oils are available at craft stores; because they are commonly used for massage therapy and aromatherapy, they are also available at health spas, beauty salons, health food stores, and bath shops. They range in scent from sweet to spicy to woodsy.

Fixatives, which absorb and retain the scents of the other materials, are a necessary ingredient in potpourri. Without fixatives, the perfume of the potpourri would be quickly lost. Orris root, calamus, and cellulose-fiber fixatives are available in craft stores and through mail-order suppliers. Some spices also make excellent fixatives, including cumin seeds, coriander, cloves, nutmeg, cinnamon, and vanilla beans. Other fixatives include frankincense, broken corn cobs, gum benzoin, cedarwood, oak moss, and oil of sandalwood. Often, more than one type of fixative is used in a potpourri blend.

Citrus blend

Wildflower blend

Pine-forest blend

Rose blend

WILDFLOWER BLEND

1 qt. (1 L) mixed dried flower petals and heads.

1 oz. (25 g) uva ursi or oregano leaves.

2 oz. (50 g) lemon verbena leaves.

4 oz. (125 g) lavender.

1 cup (250 mL) dried globe amaranth blossoms.

Small dried sunflower blossoms, optional.

10 to 12 cinnamon sticks, 3" (7.5 cm) long.

Four drops geranium essential oil.

Three drops lavender essential oil.

1 oz. (25 g) orris root powder or ¼ cup (50 mL) cut orris root, chopped calamus, or cellulose-fiber fixative.

ROSE BLEND

1 qt. (1 L) dried mixed rose petals, heads, and hips.

2 oz. (50 g) lavender.

1 cup (250 mL) dried globe amaranth blossoms.

½ teaspoon (2 mL) whole cloves.

½ teaspoon (2 mL) ground cinnamon.

Five or six star anise.

A few dried rose leaves, for color.

Four drops rose essential oil.

1 oz. (25 g) orris root powder or ¼ cup (50 mL) cut orris root, chopped calamus, or cellulose-fiber fixative.

HOW TO MAKE POTPOURRI

1 Place the fixatives and any ground spices in small bowl; add drops of essential oils. Mix thoroughly, to ensure that all the scent of the essential oil is fixed.

2 Place the remaining dry ingredients in large bowl. Set aside any decorative dried flower heads, petals, or leaves to be used as the embellishments; store them in a dry place.

3 Add the mixture in small bowl to the mixture in large bowl. Mix thoroughly, to ensure that the fixatives, essential oils, and spices are evenly distributed.

CITRUS BLEND

1 qt. (1 L) dried orange, lemon, or lime slices.

4 oz. (125 g) dried lemon peel.

2 oz. (50 g) eucalyptus leaves.

1 oz. (25 g) each of tilia and kesu flowers.

10 to 12 each of bay leaves and star anise.

10 to 12 cinnamon sticks, 3" (7.5 cm) long.

1 tablespoon (15 mL) juniper berries.

1½ teaspoons (7 mL) ground nutmeg.

Four drops citrus essential oil.

Two drops frankincense essential oil.

1 oz. (25 g) orris root powder or ¼ cup (50 mL) cut orris root, chopped calamus, or cellulose-fiber fixative.

PINE-FOREST BLEND

1 qt. (1 L) mixture of small pinecones, slivered birch bark, green eucalyptus, and princess pine and cedar needles.

½ oz. (15 g) curly pods.

10 to 15 poppy pods.

10 to 12 cinnamon sticks, 3" (7.5 cm) long.

½ teaspoon (2 mL) whole cloves.

Four drops pine essential oil.

Two drops eucalypus essential oil.

Two drops sandalwood essential oil.

1 oz. (25 g) orris root powder or ¼ cup (50 mL) cut orris root, chopped calamus, or cellulose-fiber fixative.

4 Place potpourri in airtight container; leave in dark place for at least 6 weeks. Shake the container daily for first week. The longer you store potpourri, the more its fragrance matures.

5 Place potpourri in a decorative open container. Embellish the top with the flower heads, petals, or leaves that were set aside in step 2. Reseal any potpourri that is not being used yet, in airtight container.

DECORATING WITH TOILETRIES

A wide selection of toiletries is available in bath shops, including specialty bars of soap, liquid soaps, bath crystals, and bath beads. Displayed in unique ways, these toiletries can become room accents for the bathroom. Rather than reserve these items for display only, encourage guests to help themselves by supplying a scoop for bath crystals and setting out individual portions of shaved bar soap. And set an easy-to-use decorative decanter, filled with liquid soap, next to the sink.

Specialty soaps *are partially wrapped with decorative papers and embellished with dried floral materials for an attractive display.*

Decorative bottle *contains liquid soap. Wrap the bottle neck with a pretty ribbon and add a wax seal of the host's initial.*

Evergreen-lined soap dish *makes a pretty background for a bar of herbal soap. Or use leaves, such as split-leaf philodendron, ti leaves, or leatherleaf fern.*

Bubble-gum machine *may be filled with colorful bath beads. Place a dish of pennies next to it, so guests can help themselves.*

Beach pail *for a young guest contains soap, baby shampoo, and bath toys. With the personal gift items in this guest pack, the child will look forward to bath time.*

MORE IDEAS FOR DECORATING WITH TOILETRIES

Guest boxes contain washcloths and several toiletries, including soap, bath gel, and talcum powder. Wrap the boxes with gift-wrapping paper, and decorate the lids with silk ribbons.

Curled shavings of specialty soaps, cut with a vegetable peeler, are not only decorative, but practical as well. Guests will be more inclined to use the shavings than to use a decorative bar. Display the shavings on a pretty plate next to the bars, and label the different types of soap.

Nest of excelsior, *resembling a small bird's nest, holds small molded soaps for a country room accent.*

Glass Coca Cola® bottle *(top right), used with a spout pourer, becomes a clever decanter for liquid soap or lotion soap.*

Old-fashioned candy bin *may be filled with bath crystals to accent a country bathroom. A small scoop can be used to remove the bath crystals.*

DECORATIVE BATH OILS

Bath oils, in addition to their soothing qualities, can also help to decorate the bathroom. Displayed in a special decanter and embellished with dried flowers, the clear, sparkling oils become beautiful room accents. Bath oils are easily prepared at home from sesame oil and pure essential oils, making them much more affordable than purchased bath oils.

Sesame oil, a light oil that is the main ingredient in most purchased bath oils and massage oils, is readily available at the grocery store. Sesame oils range in color from pale yellow to deep gold. To avoid any chemical additivites in the oil or the processing, select a sesame oil that is labeled 100 percent pure and naturally processed. Pure essential oils are available at craft stores, health spas, beauty salons, health food stores, and bath shops. Many types, such as lavender, jasmine, and ylang ylang, are available, each with a distinctive scent.

If you want to add dried flowers to the bath oil for embellishment, select dried flowers that have not been dyed, to prevent the possibility of the dyes bleeding into the oil. You may want to add flowers of the same variety as the essential oil, such as dried rosebuds with rose essential oil.

Use bath oil sparingly, adding 1 to 2 teaspoons (5 to 10 mL) to the water when filling the tub. Bath oil may also be used for body massages.

HOW TO MAKE DECORATIVE BATH OIL

Mix together 2 teaspoons (10 mL) pure essential oil and ½ cup (125 mL) sesame oil. Place dried flowers in a decorative decanter, if desired; fill the decanter with the prepared bath oil. Tie a ribbon bow around the neck of the decanter, if desired.

PICKET FENCE BOXES & SHELVES

The simple styling of picket fences is the basis for these clever wooden boxes and shelves. They may be used for purely decorative purposes or as practical storage accessories.

Poplar is used for both items, because it is an inexpensive hardwood with very little warpage. The wood may be distressed for an aged look or sanded smooth for a more refined look.

The overall measurement of the picket fence shelf is 11½" (29.3 cm) wide by 24½" (62.3 cm) high; it has two 12" × 3½" (30.5 × 9 cm) shelves. The overall measurement of the picket fence box is 12½" (31.8 cm) wide by 11" (28 cm) high by 5¾" (14.5 cm) deep; the inside measurement of the box is 10½" × 3½" (27.8 × 9 cm).

Picket fence styling *is featured on the display box opposite and the shelving unit above.*

HOW TO MAKE A PICKET FENCE BOX

MATERIALS

- Two ½ × 2 poplar boards, each 4 ft. (1.27 m) in length, for the pickets.
- One ½ × 4 poplar board, 4 ft. (1.27 m) in length, for the box.
- ¾" and 1" (2 and 2.5 cm) brads.
- 100-grit and 220-grit sandpaper.
- Wood glue.

- Latex or acrylic paint.
- Two swivel-type hangers and 6 × 1" (2.5 cm) brass wood screws, optional, for hanging picket fence box on wall.
- Hammer, chisel, chain, and awl, optional, for distressing wood.
- Miter box; jigsaw.

CUTTING DIRECTIONS

For the pickets, cut a ½ × 2 poplar board into four 9½" (24.3 cm) lengths and two 10½" (27.8 cm) lengths. Cut one 11½" (29.3 cm) back bar; or, if you plan to hang the picket fence box on the wall, cut two 11½" (29.3 cm) back bars.

Cut the pieces for the box from a ½ × 4 board, using a jigsaw. Cut two 3½" × 12½" (9 × 31.8 cm) pieces, for the front and back. Cut two 3½" × 3½" (9 × 9 cm) pieces, for the sides. Cut one 3½" × 10½" (9 × 27.8 cm) bottom piece.

1 Mark one end of each picket at the center, using a pencil. Cut 45° angle at marked end, cutting through marked point; repeat in the opposite direction. Save the scraps from mitering corners, to be used as spacers for the pickets.

2 Distress the wood pieces, if desired (opposite). Or, for a more refined finish, sand edges smooth, using 100-grit sandpaper and then 220-grit sandpaper.

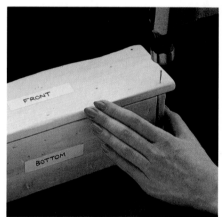

3 Position side and bottom pieces as shown, with front piece centered on top. Secure side pieces to front piece, using two 1" (2.5 cm) brads on each side; set the brads, using a nail set.

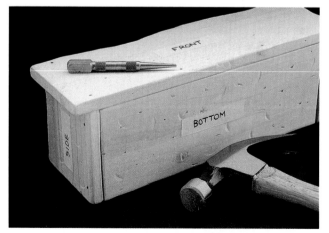

4 Secure the bottom piece to front and side pieces, using two 1" (2.5 cm) brads on front and two on each side; set the brads, using a nail set.

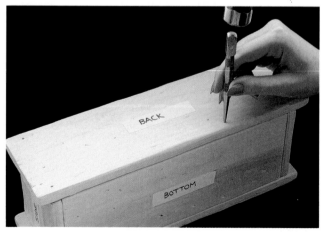

5 Position back piece, centered on sides; secure to side and bottom pieces, using 1" (2.5 cm) brads. Set the brads, using a nail set.

6 Place pickets facedown on flat surface, with 10½" (27.8 cm) pickets as the end pickets. Mark placement for lower edge of back bar, 5" (12.5 cm) from the bottom of the pickets.

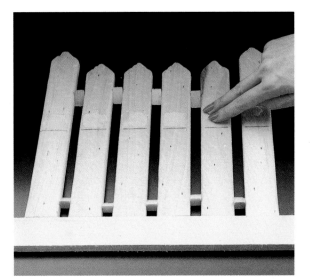

7 Place the mitered scraps between pickets as spacers; align lower edges of pickets against a scrap of wood. Where back bar will be positioned, apply wood glue sparingly; spread the wood glue with fingers.

8 Place back bar on the pickets, with lower edge on the marked lines; secure with two ¾" (2 cm) brads in each picket.

9 Secure the pickets to back of box, with back bar facing up and lower edge of pickets ½" (1.3 cm) from bottom of box, using wood glue and ¾" (2 cm) brads. Apply paint.

Hanging picket fence box. Build as in steps 1 to 9, opposite; add an extra 11½" (29.3 cm) back bar at lower end of pickets. Attach swivel hangers as on page 111, step 11.

HOW TO DISTRESS WOOD

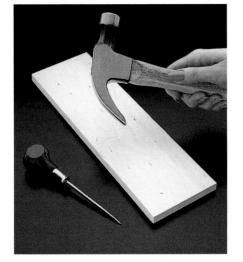

1 Pound the wood with a hammer, chisel, and chain, and pound holes randomly into wood, using an awl. Make imperfections and dents as desired.

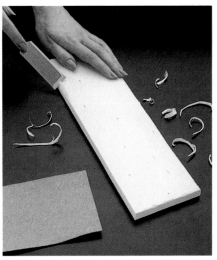

2 Complete distressed look, chiseling some edges randomly and rounding off edges, using the 100-grit sandpaper.

HOW TO MAKE A PICKET FENCE SHELF

MATERIALS

- Four ½ × 2 poplar boards, each 4 ft. (1.27 m) in length, for the pickets.
- One ½ × 4 poplar board, 2 ft. (0.63 m) in length, for the shelves and brackets.
- ¾" (2 cm) brads.
- 8 × 1¼" (3.2 cm) wood screws.
- Wood glue.

- 100-grit and 220-grit sandpaper.
- Latex or acrylic paint.
- Two swivel-type hangers and 6 × 1" (2.5 cm) brass wood screws, for hanging the shelf on the wall.
- Hammer, chisel, chain, and awl, optional, for distressing wood.
- Miter box; jigsaw; drill and ⅛" drill bit.

CUTTING DIRECTIONS

For the pickets, cut a ½ × 2 board into two 24" (61 cm) lengths and four 23" (58.5 cm) lengths, using a jigsaw. For the back bars, cut two 11½" (29.3 cm) lengths from the ½ × 2 board. For the caps on the end pickets, cut two 1½" × 2" (3.8 × 5 cm) wood pieces.

Cut the pieces for the shelves and brackets from a ½ × 4 board, using a jigsaw. Cut the board in half lengthwise to make two 3½" × 12" (9 × 30.5 cm) shelves. Cut four wooden brackets as shown in step 1.

1 Mark two 3½" (9 cm) squares on ½ × 4 board; draw a diagonal line across each square, as shown, with ends of line ½" (1.3 cm) from opposite corners. Cut on marked lines, using a jigsaw, to make four wooden brackets; set aside.

2 Cut mitered points on one end of each 23" (58.5 cm) picket, as on page 108, step 1. Sand edges smooth, using 100-grit sandpaper, then 220-grit sandpaper, for a refined look. Or distress wood pieces, if desired (page 109).

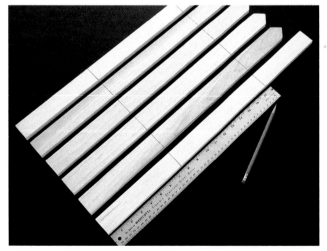

3 Place pickets facedown on a flat surface, with the 24" (61 cm) pickets as the end pickets. Mark placement lines for lower edges of back bars, 7½" and 17½" (19.3 and 44.3 cm) from bottom of pickets.

4 Place the mitered scraps between pickets as spacers; align lower edges of pickets. Where back bars will be positioned, apply wood glue sparingly; spread the glue with fingers.

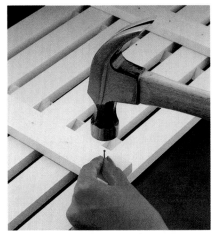

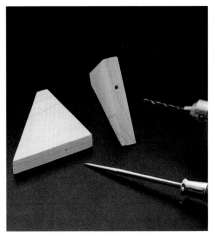

5 Place back bars on pickets, with lower edges on the marked lines; secure with one ¾" (2 cm) brad in each picket.

6 Apply wood glue sparingly to top edge of each end picket; attach a 1½" × 2" (3.8 × 5 cm) wood piece, using ¾" (2 cm) brad.

7 Mark the placement for a screw on the back edge of each bracket, 1" (2.5 cm) from the top. Centerpunch brackets with awl; predrill holes into brackets, using ⅛" drill bit.

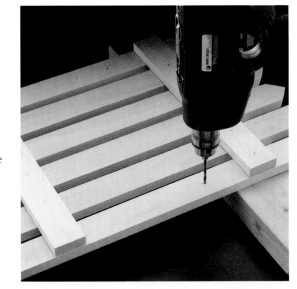

8 Mark the placement for screws on back side of end pickets, 2" (5 cm) below the back bars and centered on the pickets. Centerpunch with awl; using a ⅛" drill bit, predrill holes at marks, drilling through pickets.

9 Align brackets to pickets at predrilled holes; attach the brackets, using 8 × 1¼" (3.2 cm) wood screws. Before tightening screws, check that brackets are level.

10 Secure the shelves to the top sides of the two brackets, using wood glue and centering the shelves. Lean the shelving unit against the wall; weight down the shelves for 3 or 4 hours, until glue has dried.

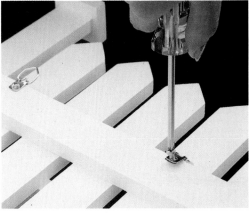

11 Apply paint. Mark screw placement for swivel hangers at top of the upper back bar, 2¾" (7 cm) from ends. Centerpunch with awl; predrill the holes, using a ⅛" drill bit. Attach swivel hangers, using 6 × 1" (2.5 cm) brass screws.

BIN & SHELVING STORAGE UNITS

These versatile wall accessories offer clever storage space for rolled hand towels, soaps, and other small items and, if desired, can provide the support for a glass or wooden shelf.

The instructions that follow are for the unit shown above, made from six pieces of lumber. The unit measures 33" (84 cm) long and 6½" (16.3 cm) high. Depending on the thickness of the backing board used, the unit has a depth of 5½" or 6¼" (14 or 15.7 cm).

The bin-and-shelving units can be custom-designed to fit the available wall space and depth in your bathroom. For smaller wall spaces, shorter units may be built by using four pieces of lumber to make two V-sections, as shown on page 117. Or, for larger wall spaces, longer shelves may be built by adding more V-sections. For even more versatility, the V-sections may graduate from smaller to larger sizes or a unit may be mounted in stair-step fashion as shown on page 117.

If you are painting the project, you may want to use medium-density fiberboard, often referred to as MDF, for the bins. Use ¼" (6 mm) hardboard as the backing board, for surfaces that sand smooth and paint well. If you want a stained wood finish, use 1 × 6 lumber for the bins and 1 × 8 lumber for the backing board.

MATERIALS

- 2 × 4 sheet of ¾" (2 cm) medium-density fiberboard or 4-ft. (1.27 m) length of 1 × 6 lumber, for the bins.

- 2 × 4 sheet of ¼" (6 mm) tempered hardboard or 3-ft. (0.95 m) length of 1 × 8 lumber, for the backing board.

- 8 × 3" (7.5 cm) nickel or brass pan-head screws and #8 finishing washers, for use with hardboard backing board; or 10 × 3" (7.5 cm) nickel or brass pan-head screws and #10 finishing washers, for use with backing board of 1 × lumber.

- ⅜" (1 cm) dowel, for the plugs.

- #8 × 1⅝" (4 cm) coarse-thread drywall screws.

- Wood glue.

- Awl; chisel.

- Sanding block; 80-grit and 220-grit sandpaper.

- Plastic toggles, if unit is not mounted into wall studs.

- Clamp, such as a pipe clamp.

- Drill; ⅛" combination drill and countersink bit; ⅜" drill bit.

- Jigsaw, circular saw, or backsaw and miter box.

- Coping saw or other small saw.

- Acrylic or latex paint, or wood stain and clear acrylic finish.

CUTTING DIRECTIONS

From the medium-density fiberboard or 1 × 6 lumber, cut the pieces for the bins. Cut one piece 5½" × 8¼" (14 × 21.2 cm); label it Piece A in a light pencil marking. Cut all five remaining pieces 5½" × 7½" (14 × 19.3 cm); in the steps that follow, these are referred to as Pieces B through F. The backing board is cut on page 114, steps 5 and 6.

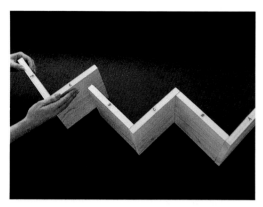

1 Position the pieces on table as they will be assembled, to check the fit and layout, positioning Piece A to the far right. Pieces are referred to as A through F, from right to left.

2 Clamp Piece A and Piece B together at right angles, using a clamp, with Piece B lying flat on table. Mark placement for two screws on Piece A, ⅜" (1 cm) from lower edge and 1" (2.5 cm) from each side; also mark the placement for third screw, at center, ⅜" (1 cm) from lower edge. Centerpunch holes at markings, using an awl.

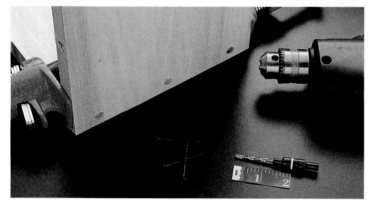

3 Adjust ⅛" combination drill and countersink bit for 2" (5 cm) depth as shown; tighten set screw. Drill holes through Piece A and into Piece B; counterbore holes up to point on bit indicated by white line. Insert #8 × 1⅝" (4 cm) drywall screws.

4 Clamp Piece B and Piece C together at right angles, with Piece C flat on table. Mark screw holes on Piece B as for Piece A in step 2; drill the screw holes and insert screws as in step 3. Repeat for remaining pieces D through F.

5 Lay unit on backing board, with upper points even with edge of backing board; trace outer cutting line on backing board, and trace all edges of lumber.

6 Cut backing board on the outer cutting lines. Mark lines on front side of the backing board to indicate where pieces are screwed together, as shown; indicate 2" (5 cm) length of screws on backing board.

7 Mark placement for screws on the front side of backing board; avoid areas where the previous screws are inserted, as indicated by markings from step 6. Centerpunch the holes; drill holes through backing board at placement marks, using ⅛" drill bit.

8 Place unit on table, with the front edge facing down. Turn backing board over, and place on top of unit, aligning edges.

9 Predrill hole for middle screw into the unit, using a ⅛" combination drill and countersink bit, keeping unit aligned with the backing board; countersink the hole up to point on bit indicated by white line. Screw through backing board and into unit, using drywall screw.

10 Predrill holes and insert one end screw as in step 9, rechecking alignment; repeat for opposite end screw.

11 Predrill holes in unit for all remaining screws. Insert screws.

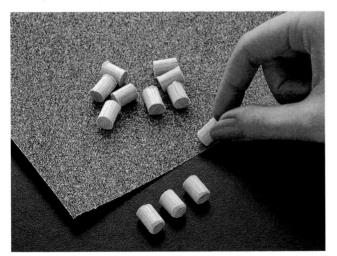

12 Cut ½" (1.3 cm) piece of dowel for each screw hole, for the plugs. To bevel one end of each plug, sand or file edge slightly. This makes it easier to insert the plugs into the drilled holes.

13 Apply a small amount of wood glue into holes, using cotton swab. Tap plugs into holes as far as possible, using hammer or wooden mallet; the fit will be quite snug. Wipe any excess glue, using a dampened wool cloth. Allow to dry overnight.

(Continued)

14 Sand outer edges of backing board and edges of shelves. Cut off excess plugs after glue has thoroughly dried, so plugs extend slightly; use small saw, and take care not to scratch wood surface.

15 Sand plugs flush with surface, using 80-grit sandpaper on a sanding block. Sand the unit, using 220-grit sandpaper. Paint the unit, or apply stain and clear acrylic finish.

16 Mark placement of screws for hanging unit on front side of backing board, centered in each "V" area of unit and 1" (2.5 cm) down from upper edge of backing board. Predrill holes, using ⅛" drill bit.

17 Position unit on wall; tap small nail into wall through one screw hole.

18 Place a carpenter's level on top of unit. With nail holding the unit at one end, slide opposite end up and down until unit is leveled. Mark placement for screw at the opposite end, using nail.

19 Drill holes for plastic toggles into wall at placement marks. If there is a wall stud at placement mark, toggle is not needed. Tap plastic toggles into drilled holes, using hammer.

20 Reposition the unit. At each hole, insert pan-head screw through finishing washer and then through hole in unit; screw into toggle. At wall stud, screw into a predrilled hole without a toggle.

MORE IDEAS FOR BIN & SHELVING STORAGE UNITS

Decorative backing board is cut oversized and has rounded corners. Construct the unit as on pages 114 to 116, steps 1 to 20, cutting the backing board to the desired shape and size in steps 5 and 6. The backing board and the edges are painted in a darker color than the sides of the shelves.

Diagonal shelving unit is made from a 1 × 8 board, cut into graduated lengths; from right to left, the end piece is 8¼" (21.2 cm) long, the second piece is 7½" (19.3 cm) long, the next two are 6½" (16.3 cm) long, and the next two are 5½" (14 cm) long. Construct the unit as on pages 114 to 116, steps 1 to 16, and hang the unit diagonally on the wall.

DECORATING WITH SILK FLOWERS

F loral arrangements add softness and color to the bathroom. Depending on the space available, choose either a nosegay or a vase arrangement for display on the countertop, or a wall swag.

For either arrangement, silk flowers are recommended over dried naturals, because they are unaffected by humidity. They are also more easily cleaned, an important consideration in humid rooms where moist dust particles tend to collect readily. Avoid using silk flowers that have paper-wrapped stems, because they are not washable.

SILK FLORAL BOUQUETS

The vase arrangement is constructed as a hand-tied bouquet. With this method, the silk flowers are clustered and wrapped with wire, eliminating the need for any floral foam, which tends to absorb odors. Following the same basic principles as those for arranging fresh flowers, make the bouquet either triangular or rounded in shape. A hand-tied bouquet may be embellished with a ribbon bow and used as a nosegay on the countertop, rather than placed in a vase.

For cleaning, simply remove the entire hand-tied bouquet from the vase or untie the ribbon of the nosegay. Then wash the bouquet in lukewarm water, and allow it to air dry.

SILK FLORAL SWAG

A floral swag may be hung either vertically or horizontally on the wall. Even small bathrooms usually have a vertical wall space to embellish decoratively, or a horizontal area above the towel bar, mirror, or medicine cabinet.

Easily constructed, this floral swag is simply wired together, without the need for a floral form.

Choose silk flowers with flexible stems. Select large focal flowers with thick stems to provide a sturdy base for the swag.

Vase of silk flowers *adds a display of soft color on a countertop.*

Floral swag (above) may hang horizontally over a towel bar or a mirror. Or, if preferred, the swag may hang vertically on a narrow wall space.

Hand-tied bouquet (left) is embellished with a pretty bow from organza ribbon.

HOW TO MAKE A SILK FLORAL BOUQUET

MATERIALS

- Silk flowering branches or other line materials.
- Silk magnolias or other large focal flowers.
- Silk alstroemeria or other medium-size secondary flowers.

- Additional silk flowers, for filler material.
- Container, such as ceramic vase.
- 22-gauge paddle floral wire; wire cutter.

1 **Vase arrangement.** Hold a flowering branch next to vase; cut stem to desired height for tallest floral materials, using wire cutter.

2 Place first flowering branch on the table. On each side, place another flowering branch, shorter than the first. Wire stems together at a point that will be lower than rim of vase, using paddle wire.

3 Layer two or three more flowering branches, with flowers shorter than the previous flowers; wire stems together.

4 Wire the magnolia stems over the flowering branches, one stem at a time, with each flower shorter than the previous flower and wrapping tightly with wire.

5 Add the alstroemeria stems, one at a time, evenly spacing them throughout arrangement; wrap tightly with wire. Repeat for filler material in any bare areas.

6 Arrange bouquet in hand, bending stems to add softness and depth to the arrangement. Cut excess length from stems to match desired height of original flower. Place in vase.

7 Place marbles around the stems, covering wire, if clear vase is used. Or plastic wrap may be used to hold stems in place, if vase is opaque.

Nosegay. Follow steps 1 to 6, above, ignoring references to the vase. Wrap the ribbon around the wires; tie a bow.

HOW TO MAKE A SILK FLORAL WALL SWAG

MATERIALS

- Silk lilies or other line material with large flowers.
- Silk roses or other medium-size focal materials.
- Cluster of berries and other fruit or other secondary materials.
- Silk grapevine leaves or other greenery, for filler material.
- 22-gauge paddle floral wire; wire cutter.

1 Place two lilies on table, aligning stems in opposite directions and overlapping them; wire the stems together, using paddle wire. Shape stems for a natural appearance.

2 Add desired number of lilies on each side, wiring one stem at a time. As each flower is added, shape stem for a natural appearance. Wire will be concealed later.

3 Wire stems of roses, one at a time, evenly spacing them throughout swag and wrapping wire tightly; shape the stems.

4 Add stems of berries and other fruit, one stem at a time, evenly spacing them throughout arrangement; wrap tightly with wire.

5 Cut short stems of silk grapevine leaves or other leaves, placing them throughout swag to conceal wires and stems of flowers and to soften the look; wire in place.

6 Shape a small wire loop; wrap wire ends around some of the stems to secure loop on the back, for hanging. For horizontal swag, position wire loop at center back; for vertical swag, position loop under the top focal flower, securing it to a heavy stem.

7 Shape the swag as necessary. Hang swag from a wire loop.

CONTAINER GARDENS & TERRARIUMS

Live plants add softness to a predominantly hard-surfaced bathroom. For an ever-changing room accent, they can be grown in a container garden or terrarium. Plants can thrive in the bathroom, provided the plant varieties are carefully selected according to the bathroom's environment. Refer to the chart on page 124 for recommended varieties. Bathrooms provide more humidity than other rooms in the house, which is a healthier environment for many plants. Many bathrooms, however, are low in light, limiting the selection of suitable plants. If the bathroom has insufficient light, make two container gardens or terrariums, rotating them periodically from a well-lit room to the bathroom.

CONTAINER GARDENS

Container gardens are essentially a grouping of plants growing together in a single container, such as a ceramic dish or a basket. A European dish garden has a blooming plant added to the grouping. For a pleasing variety, select plants of varying heights and include one or more plants that vine, such as ivy and philodendron. Choose plants that complement each other, such as spiky plants mixed with bushy plants, and dark green plants mixed with variegated ones.

African violets are a good choice for European dish gardens, because they bloom for about six weeks and like humidity. Although they need high light until they bloom, they can then be placed in a room with less light. Other blooming plants are included on the chart on page 124.

Select a container at least 3" (7.5 cm) deep. If the container has drainage holes, keep a saucer under it to catch the excess water; if it does not have drainage holes, prepare the container with charcoal and rocks (page 124). A basket may be used for a container garden, provided it has a plastic liner.

Water the container garden as necessary to keep the soil moist to the touch, using either spring water or hard water; soft water should not be used, because it contains salt. For healthy plant growth, fertilize the plants, using a fertilizer recommended by the greenhouse.

TERRARIUMS

Terrariums thrive on moisture. The plants are nestled in a glass goldfish bowl to create a greenhouse environment. Plant a terrarium as you would a container garden, using charcoal and rock in the bottom of the bowl. As an additional design element, decorative rocks, coral, shells, bark, or small twigs may be added to the terrarium.

Select a variety of slow-growing plants that will not quickly outgrow the confined space. Popular varieties for terrariums include peperomia, baby's tears, Venus flytrap, podocarpus, and maidenhair fern. Small palms and orchids may also be used, although they tend to grow large. Select the varieties that are suitable for the light level in the bathroom (page 124). Care for a terrarium by watering and fertilizing it as you would a container garden, above.

PLANT VARIETIES SUITABLE FOR CONTAINER GARDENS & TERRARIUMS

LIGHT CONDITIONS	CONTAINER GARDENS	TERRARIUMS
LOW LIGHT	Cast-iron plant; China doll; Chinese evergreen; Dallas fern; maidenhair fern; moss; Neanthe Bella palm; all varieties of philodendron; podocarpus; silver queen. Blooming plants include anthurium and spathiphyllum, also known as peace plant. African violets may be placed in low light once they are in bloom.	Baby's tears; small bamboo palm; moss; all varieties of peperomia; podocarpus; maidenhair fern.
MEDIUM LIGHT	Asparagus fern; bamboo palm; birdsnest fern; Bolivian Jew; Boston fern; button fern; all varieties of dracaena; fluffy ruffles fern; Hawaiian ti; nephthytis; oak leaf ivy; all varieties of peperomia; podocarpus; pothos; prayer plant; ribbon plant; spider plant; Swedish ivy; wandering Jew; white fittonia. African violets may be placed in medium light once they are in bloom.	Baby's tears; small bamboo palm; all varieties of peperomia; podocarpus; Venus flytrap.
HIGH LIGHT	Aloe; Areca palm; croton; dwarf pineapple; most varieties of ivy; ming Aralia. Blooming plants include African violet; bromeliad; cyclamen; orchid.	Venus flytrap; orchid.

HOW TO MAKE A CONTAINER GARDEN OR TERRARIUM

MATERIALS

- Several plant varieties in varying heights, suitable for humidity and light level of the bathroom.
- Container at least 3" (7.5 cm) deep; clear glass goldfish bowl, for terrarium.
- Crushed charcoal and river rocks or marble rocks, for use in terrarium or any container without drainage holes.
- Potting soil.
- Moss, optional.
- Embellishments, such as seashells, coral, decorative rocks, bark, or twigs, for terrarium.

1 Pour ½" (1.3 cm) layer of crushed charcoal in the bottom of container, then ½" (1.3 cm) layer of river rocks or of marble rocks, if container does not have drainage holes.

2 Pour 1" (2.5 cm) layer of potting soil on top of the rocks.

3 Remove plants carefully from original pots, holding plant upside down and gently pulling it from container.

4 Arrange plants in the prepared container, nestling them together and surrounding them with potting soil. Plant taller plants toward the back and shorter ones toward the front. Take care not to overcrowd the plants, to allow room for the roots to grow.

5 Fill in remaining space with potting soil. Water the garden until the potting soil is moderately saturated.

6 Cover soil with moss, if desired. Use paintbrush to brush away any soil on leaves or container. Check the moisture level in 24 hours.

European dish garden. Follow steps 1 to 6, opposite, except do not remove blooming plant from its original pot; nestle the potted plant with other plants in the garden. When blooming has stopped, the plant may be replaced with a fresh blooming plant.

Terrarium. Follow steps 1 to 6, opposite, using clear glass goldfish bowl as the container. After plants are in place, add desired design elements, such as seashells, coral, decorative rocks, bark, or twigs.

INDEX

CREDITS

CY DECOSSE INCORPORATED

Chairman/CEO: Philip L. Penny
Chairman Emeritus: Cy DeCosse
President/COO: Nino Tarantino
Executive V.P./Editor-in-Chief:
  William B. Jones

DECORATING THE BATHROOM
Created by: The Editors of
Cy DeCosse Incorporated

Also available from the publisher:
Bedroom Decorating, Creative Window
Treatments, Decorating for Christmas,
Decorating the Living Room, Creative
Accessories for the Home, Decorating
with Silk & Dried Flowers, Decorating
the Kitchen, Decorative Painting,
Decorating Your Home for Christmas,
Decorating for Dining & Entertaining,
Decorating with Fabric & Wallcovering,
Decorating with Great Finds, Affordable
Decorating, Picture-Perfect Walls, More
Creative Window Treatments, Outdoor
Decor, The Gift of Christmas

Group Executive Editor: Zoe A. Graul
Senior Technical Director: Rita C. Arndt
Senior Project Manager: Kristen Olson
Assistant Project Manager: Elaine
  Johnson

Associate Creative Director:
  Lisa Rosenthal
Art Director: Stephanie Michaud
Writer: Rita C. Arndt
Editor: Janice Cauley
Researcher/Designer: Michael Basler
Researcher: Linda Neubauer
Sample Supervisor: Carol Olson
Senior Technical Photo Stylist:
  Bridget Haugh
Technical Photo Stylists: Susan Pasqual,
  Nancy Sundeen
Styling Director: Bobbette Destiche
Crafts Stylists: Jill Engelhart, Coralie
  Sathre
Prop Assistant/Shopper: Margo Morris
Artisans: Arlene Dohrman, Sharon
  Ecklund, Corliss Forstrom, Phyllis
  Galbraith, Valerie Hill, Kristi Kuhnau,
  Virginia Mateen, Carol Pilot, Michelle
  Skudlarek, Nancy Sundeen
Vice President of Development Planning
  & Production: Jim Bindas
Director of Photography: Mike Parker
Creative Photo Coordinator: Cathleen
  Shannon
Studio Manager: Marcia Chambers
Lead Photographer: Mike Parker
Photographers: Stuart Block, Rebecca
  Hawthorne, Kevin Hedden, Rex Irmen,
  William Lindner, Mark Macemon, Paul
  Najlis, Charles Nields, Greg Wallace
Contributing Photographers: Phil
  Aarestad, Kim Bailey, Paul Englund,
  Mette Nielsen, Brad Parker, Steve Smith

Production Manager: Laurie Gilbert
Desktop Publishing Specialist:
  Laurie Kristensen
Production Staff: Deborah Eagle, Kevin
  Hedden, Jeff Hickman, Jeanette Moss,
  Michelle Peterson, Mike Schauer, Kay
  Wethern, Nik Wogstad
Shop Supervisor: Phil Juntti
Scenic Carpenters: Rob Johnstone, John
  Nadeau, Greg Wallace
Consultants: Katie Guyer Donovan,
  Amy Engman, Wendy Fedie, Patrick
  Kartes, Katie King, Nadine Millot,
  Mike Palkowitsch
Contributors: American Olean Tile
  Company; Armstrong Flooring; Conso
  Products Company; Dritz Corporation;
  EZ International; Fabby Custom
  Lighting; Formica Corp.; General
  Marble; Graber Industries, Inc.; Kirsch;
  Macy's; Plaid Enterprises; Swiss-
  Metrosene, Inc.; Untapped Resource-
  Sheryl Vanderpol; Waverly, Division
  of F. Schumacher & Company
Printed on American paper by:
R. R. Donnelley & Sons Co.

99 98 97 96 / 5 4 3 2 1

Cy DeCosse Incorporated offers
a variety of how-to books. For
information write:
  Cy DeCosse Subscriber Books
  5900 Green Oak Drive
  Minnetonka, MN 55343